THE NATION'S
REPORT CARD
naep

The Writing Report Card

Writing Achievement in American Schools

by Arthur N. Applebee
Judith A. Langer   Ina V. S. Mullis

November 1986

Report No: 15-W-02

Table of Contents

Writing Objectives:
To enhance students' ability to express themselves appropriately and effectively, to develop their ability to think and also to develop an attitude of enriching their lives through their positive expressions.

National Course of Study. **Japan, 1983**

When report cards are brought home across America, many disappointed parents exhort their children to "try harder."

This *Writing Report Card* also demands that kind of response.

While no organization in the United States is specifically charged with the responsibility of setting the kind of national standard placed before Japanese teachers, none of us can be comfortable with this report's emphasis on "minimal and adequate." Performance in writing in our schools is, quite simply, *bad.* The skills of the nation's schoolchildren fall far short of the high standards called for in *A Nation at Risk.*

For parents, an important part of this report will be those sections describing the links between achievement and home environment. For teachers, the relationship between instructional practice and student performance may provide some clues to improvement.

Well over 60 percent of America's 110 million salaried workers generate written material on a regular basis (Office of Technology Assessment). In view of the results reported here, one has to wonder just how "appropriately and effectively" they all communicate.

In these pages, students acknowledge the importance of writing but candidly express their dislike for the subject. Most of them do not appear to have the ability to "enrich their lives through their positive expressions." Both parents and teachers share the burden of developing children's enthusiasm for this important skill.

The hope is that these findings will suggest directions to those interested in setting writing objectives for the thousands of schools in America.

Archie E. Lapointe
Executive Director

The National Assessment of Educational Progress, *The Nation's Report Card*, is funded by the Office for Educational Research and Improvement—Center for Statistics, under a grant to Educational Testing Service. National Assessment is an education research project mandated by Congress to collect data over time on the perfomance of young Americans in various learning areas. It makes available information on assessment procedures to state and local education agencies.

This report, No. 15-W-02, can be ordered from the National Assessment of Educational Progress at Educational Testing Service, Rosedale Road, Princeton, New Jersey 08541-0001.

Library of Congress, Catalog Card Number: *86-62418*

ISBN *0-88685-055X*

The work upon which this publication is based was performed pursuant to Grant No. NIE-G-83-0011 of the Office for Educational Research and Improvement. It does not, however, necessarily reflect the views of that agency.

Educational Testing Service is an equal opportunity/affirmative action employer.

Chapter

Summary and Implications

This report is based on NAEP's 1984 national assessment of the writing achievement of American school children.* The assessment was administered to nationally representative samples of fourth-, eighth-, and eleventh-grade students attending public and private schools across the nation. Nearly 55,000 students participated in this assessment; and at least 90,000 written responses to writing tasks were available for analysis.

NAEP assessed informative, persuasive, and imaginative writing performance by asking students to complete job applications, descriptions, reports, analyses, letters, stories, and other writing tasks. Fifteen different writing tasks were given to students at each grade level, but no student responded to more than four of these relatively brief writing assignments, with a national probability sample of about 2,000 students responding to each task.

Students' success was evaluated in terms of the specific goal of each writing assignment. Papers were judged to be **unsatisfactory, minimal, adequate,** or **elaborated**; when illegible or otherwise unscorable, they were **not rated**. Specific definitions of these ratings were developed for each item, and readers with experience in the teaching of writing were trained on sample responses until all were comfortable with the guidelines. Twenty percent of the responses were judged by two readers, and the percentages of *exact* agreement ranged from 88 to 96 percent at grade 4, 78 to 90 percent at grade 8, and 88 to 95 percent at grade 11. While the guidelines for evaluating specific tasks are discussed in more detail elsewhere in the report, general definitions that hold across all writing tasks follow.

*A previously published report, *Writing Trends Across the Decade, 1974-84*, contains information on changes in writing achievement across the school years ending in 1974, 1979, and 1984. That report is confined to the results for a subset of the writing tasks given to students in 1984—those that were administered using identical procedures across at least two assessments.

Levels of Writing Task Accomplishment

Not Rated. A small percentage of the responses were blank, undecipherable, totally off task, or contained a statement to the effect that the student did not know how to do the task; these responses were not rated.

Unsatisfactory. Students writing papers judged as unsatisfactory provided very abbreviated, circular, or disjointed responses that did not represent even a basic beginning toward addressing the writing task. The following letter asking for a summer job helping out at a local swimming pool is an example:

I want to work in the pool.

Minimal. Students writing at the minimal level recognized some or all of the elements needed to complete the task, but did not manage the elements well enough to assure the purpose of the task would be achieved. The following letter of application is an example:

I have been experence at cleaning house. I've also work at a pool be for I love keeping things neat organized and clean I'm very social I'll get to know peopl really fast. I never forget to do things

Adequate. Adequate responses included the information and ideas critical to accomplishing the underlying task and were considered likely to be effective in achieving the desired purpose. The following letter was judged adequate:

I feel that I would be a very good choice for this job. I'm very responsible and I like to work with kids. I will do my best to be polite and to make the visitors want to return again. I would enjoy and appreciate this job very much. I would never be late and I would even work overtime to clean up if it's needed. I worked at a swimming pool last summer so I've had past experience in this area. I realize that there are many young people who want this job. I would appreciate it if you would consider me

Elaborated. Occasionally responses went beyond the essential, reflecting a higher level of coherence and providing more supporting detail; these responses were identified as elaborated.

My name is Tracy, and I have just graduated from my junior year of high school. I feel that I am a very capable and responsible person for the job. Proof of this is seen during my junior year. I held down a very important and responsible job being the editor of the school yearbook. This was no easy task, but I got the job done meeting every deadline. That brings up another point, my punctuality. If I can meet demanding yearbook deadlines with no help from my various staffs, I can easily get to my job on time.

I am also an experienced swimmer. I had swimming lessons starting at the age of 4. I also have much experience vaccuuming a pool. I know how important the upkeep of a swimming pool is and how costly it can be. I follow the rules of no running horseplay, or anything glass are to be around the swimming pool.

I also have plenty experience handling customers, for I have held down a part time job for almost seven months now. I deal with customers every day, but the good thing about that, is that I like it.

I think I am very qualified for your position that you are offering, and I hope that you will consider me for the job.

NOTE: These guidelines emphasize such features as content, logic, and development. A separate publication will present results for writing mechanics.

In addition to the writing tasks, students responded to a series of questions about their writing-related experiences, the kinds of things they were asked to write in school, and the kinds of help their teachers provided. These responses were used to develop a profile of home and school writing experiences and to examine relationships between particular background factors and writing achievement.

This first chapter presents an overview of selected findings of interest to the general public. The remainder of the report is divided into two major sections:

Part I describes writing achievement for each of the three broadly defined types of writing that students were asked to do. Chapters 2 through 4 report national performance on the informative, persuasive, and imaginative writing tasks. Chapter 5 describes the average writing achievement for the nation, for ethnic/racial and other demographic subgroups, and for various home background factors.

Part II presents findings that relate student responses to questions about their writing practices and instruction to their achievement in writing. Chapter 6 examines students' values and attitudes toward writing and relates them to writing achievement. Chapter 7 discusses the strategies and approaches that students use when they write. Chapter 8 discusses students' reports on instruction—what they write and the kinds of help provided by their teachers.

A Procedural Appendix is included for those who wish further technical information.

Highlights of the 1984 Assessment

The results presented in the chapters that follow provide an overall portrait of the writing achievement of American students in grades 4, 8, and 11. This portrait is not flattering: Most students, majority and minority alike, are unable to write **adequately** except in response to the simplest of tasks. Although writing performance improves from grade 4 to grade 8—and less dramatically from grade 8 to grade 11—even at grade 11, fewer than one-fourth of the students performed **adequately** on writing tasks involving skills required for success in academic studies, business, or the professions. In general, American students can write at a **minimal** level, but cannot express themselves well enough to ensure that their writing will accomplish the intended purpose.

- Analytic writing was difficult for students in all grades. Even on the easiest task, which asked students to compare and contrast, only 25 percent of the eleventh graders, 18 percent of the eighth graders, and 2 percent of the fourth graders wrote **adequate** or better analyses.

  Many students, however, appeared to know the basic elements of analytic writing. Eighty-five percent of the eleventh graders and 81 percent of the eighth graders wrote responses to this task at the **minimal** level or better. At fourth grade, fewer than half the students attained the **minimal** level.

- In persuasive writing, students had difficulty providing evidence for their points of view. Fewer than one-third of all students assessed on any persuasive task wrote responses judged **adequate** or better. Even in eleventh grade, only 28 percent wrote **adequate** or **elaborated** responses to the least difficult persuasive task.

  On the other hand, most students were able to express their points of view. Ninety percent of the eleventh graders and 85 percent of the eighth graders were able to complete the easiest persuasive tasks at or above the **minimal** level of performance. Even at fourth grade, two-thirds of the students completed a simple persuasive task at or above the **minimal** level.

- Students had less difficulty with tasks requiring short responses based on personal experience. Sixty-five percent of the eleventh-grade students wrote an **adequate** or better description for a job application. Less than 19 percent of the eighth graders and 2 percent of the fourth graders wrote **adequate** or better responses to a similar task.

  Most students, however, were able to provide some information about their experiences. Substantial proportions of the fourth-grade (73 percent), eight-grade (89 percent), and eleventh-grade (81 percent) students were able to write at least **minimal** responses to tasks asking for reports based on personal experience.

- Students found it moderately difficult to write well-developed stories. About 48 percent of the eleventh graders and 33 percent of the eighth graders wrote stories judged as **adequate** or better. Less than 9 percent of the fourth graders wrote stories at or above the **adequate** level.

Almost all the students, however, understood the elements of story writing. In response to the simplest story-writing task, 81 percent of the fourth graders, 89 percent of the eighth graders, and approximately 90 percent of the eleventh graders were able to write at the **minimal** level or better.

Additional Findings

Although NAEP data do not establish cause-and-effect relationships, results also show that:

- Writing performance was higher for White and Asian-American students than for Black and Hispanic students, for females than for males, and for students from advantaged-urban communities than for those from disadvantaged-urban communities.

- Home environment is related to writing achievement. Students whose parents have a post-high-school education and those with more reading materials in their homes have higher writing achievement.

- Better readers tend to have higher writing achievement; students who did well on National Assessment measures of reading proficiency also did well on measures of writing achievement.

- Students who reported writing three or more reports and essays during a six-week period had higher achievement levels than students who reported doing no writing during that time period. Although only 22 percent of the fourth graders, 12 percent of the eighth graders, and 9 percent of the eleventh graders reported doing *no* writing, nearly half the fourth graders (48 percent) and more than one-third of the eighth and eleventh graders (38 and 37 percent, respectively) reported writing fewer than three reports or essays during a six-week period.

- Students who report doing more planning, revising, and editing are better writers than those who report doing less. However, NAEP results indicate that instruction in the writing process has little relationship to student achievement.

- Students' positive attitudes toward writing deteriorate steadily across the grades. In grade 4, 57 percent of the students report that they like to write. This falls to 39 percent by the eleventh grade.

- Students report that their teachers are more likely to mark mistakes than to show an interest in what they write or to make suggestions for the next paper.

- Students' reports on the types of writing they do in school indicate an increasing emphasis on academic writing in the high school years, accompanied by a restriction in the range of other types of writing.

- Writing for subjects other than English increases between grades 4 and 8, but decreases again in senior high school.

Reflections

One of the most distressing findings is the continuing difficulty older students have explaining and defending their ideas. Even at grade 11, relatively few students were able to provide **adequate** responses to analytic writing tasks, and fewer still were able to muster arguments to persuade others to accept their points of view. That the eleventh graders were, for the most part, able to provide **minimal** responses to the persuasive and analytic tasks indicates a basic understanding of what is required in such writing. What these students seemed to lack were strategies for fulfilling those requirements. In a persuasive task, for example, their writing was likely to reflect the need to take a stand and support it with evidence, but the evidence that they cited was unresponsive to the concerns of their readers, disorganized, or unelaborated. Rather than using coherent arguments or explanations, far too many students resorted to simple lists or catalogs of related information.

Students did produce their responses under the restraints of usual testing rather than instructional conditions—limited time, artificial tasks, lack of feedback, and no provision for revising their work at some later time. Thus, their assessment responses are first-draft efforts, and it is reasonable to expect that first drafts would be less well organized and contain fewer well-developed ideas than later drafts. The scoring guidelines for the assessment, however, made allowances for these restraints.

A major conclusion to draw from this assessment is that students at all grade levels are deficient in higher-order thinking skills. The findings indicate that students have difficulty performing adequately on analytic writing tasks, as well as on persuasive tasks that ask them to defend and support their opinions. Some of these problems may reflect a pervasive lack of instructional emphasis on developing higher-order skills in all areas of the curriculum. Because writing and thinking are so deeply intertwined, appropriate writing assignments provide an ideal way to increase students' experiences with such types of thinking.

That students are having such difficulty organizing their thoughts coherently in writing suggests that they need much further guidance in how to think about what they write. As discussed below, two major national movements in the teaching of writing seem to hold promise in addressing this issue and providing direction for what can be done.

- **Students need broad-based experiences in which reading and writing tasks are integrated into their work throughout the curriculum.**

In recent years, "writing across the curriculum" has become a byword of curriculum change, replete with mandates for teachers of all subjects and at all grade levels to provide students with frequent opportunities to engage in extended writing about the material they are studying. This has occurred in response to reports that schoolchildren were not writing *often* enough, that the limited writing they were doing was not *lengthy* enough, and that the topics they were writing about were not *thoughtful* enough. Indeed, previous reports have suggested that most school writing consists of exercises that call for writing with no purpose other than practice. Many years of research suggest that better learning occurs when students *use* writing to think about what they are learning in their various classes. The relationship between reading proficiency and writing achievement also emphasizes the integrated nature of reading and writing skills.

The 1984 assessment examined general skills that should be fostered throughout the school curriculum. Many of the tasks drew upon science or social studies material or common life experiences, while others required skills in reporting, summarizing, and examining ideas that are essential to success in any job-related or academic subject. That students have so much difficulty with many of these tasks should be of concern to all educators, not just to teachers of English. Indeed, the only tasks in the assessment that might be thought of primarily as the concern of teachers of English and language arts were the imaginative writing tasks—and those are among the tasks on which students did best. All three types of writing, however, showed wide variation in the level of difficulty of individual items, reflecting the broad range of skills that students need to develop as they become competent writers. Rather than a sequence of skills that begins in imaginative writing and moves toward persuasive, the results of this assessment suggest that development continues within each of these three broad types of work throughout the school years—and probably well beyond.

■ **Instruction in the writing process needs to focus on teaching students how to think more effectively as they write.**

In the 1970s, the emphasis in writing instruction moved from the final product to the process—planning, drafting, revising, and editing.* As a result, school districts across the country have begun to institute process-oriented approaches to writing instruction. This grows out of previous research (supported further in this report) indicating that better writers have flexible ways of getting their work done—they generate, plan, organize, monitor, revise, reformulate, and review the papers they are writing. Process-oriented instruction encourages all students to use these writing techniques.

Student reports do suggest that process-oriented instructional activities have begun to be incorporated into classrooms across the nation, although not in the majority of classrooms. Some students did report extensive exposure to process-oriented writing activities, yet the achievement of these students was not consistently higher or lower than the achievement of those who did not receive such instruction. At all three grade levels assessed, students who said their teachers regularly encouraged process-related activities wrote about as well as students who said their teachers did not.

On the other hand, whether students learn these writing techniques through formal instruction or not, those who use them do write better. NAEP results show that older students and better writers plan, revise, and edit more frequently than younger students and poorer writers. The better writers are using aspects of the writing process and are performing better than students who report less frequent use of planning, revising, and editing techniques.

Since students who plan, revise, and edit are more likely to be better writers, the NAEP results support the national emphasis on teaching the writing process. Students who use the kinds of process strategies we think teachers should be teaching have higher writing achievement. The results, however, do not indicate that classroom instruction in the writing process has been effective. This suggests that the new

*"Teaching Writing," *The Harvard Education Letter*, September, 1985.

instructional approaches are treating the writing process in a superficial manner. Students are not learning to link process activities with the problems they face in their own writing. To be effective, writing instruction must focus on and clarify these links.

In summary, both of these reform movements—writing across the curriculum and process-oriented instruction—seem educationally sound; they make common sense and research sense. They have been embraced by many teachers, administrators, teacher trainers, and policy planners because they do make sense. Yet, recent research as well as the results of this assessment suggest that the changes in instruction that have occurred thus far have had no appreciable effect on student learning. Although some of the writing activities students engage in have changed, these changes have not led to adequate levels of writing achievement.

Why is this so? Because the changes are recent, the new approaches to instruction may not be well enough understood and their implications not fully enough explored. Many of the changes may be superficial, affecting *what* students are being asked to do (the outward surface of classroom activity) without making clear *how* these activities relate to what students are learning about writing. It is the *how* that should be at the heart of the movement to reform writing instruction.

What can be done? The focus needs to shift, with attention paid not merely to the activities themselves, but to teaching students ways to *think* as they write. If they are to improve their ability to communicate effectively, students must be encouraged to seek the help and information they need to formulate their ideas more clearly and to express these ideas accurately in writing. The art of successful teaching of writing involves helping students think about what to do and how to do it as they are engaged in the process of writing—and students need this kind of support in all their subjects, each and every day.

Part I

How Well Students Write: Results for the Nation and Selected Subgroups

Writing tasks in the 1984 assessment were designed to assess students' ability to engage in three broad types of writing: informative, persuasive, and imaginative. Informative writing is used to present information and ideas, including reporting about science experiments and books, describing or explaining newly researched material, and discussing analyses of situations or concepts. Persuasive writing attempts to influence others to bring about some action or change. Regardless of the issue, writers must first be concerned with having an effect on their readers beyond simply adding to their knowledge of a particular topic. The imaginative writing tasks asked students to write stories in which they reshape reality or invent plausible or implausible events or to project themselves into a particular situation and express the feelings and thoughts that it provokes.

Chapter 2 presents results from the informative writing tasks; Chapters 3 and 4 present results from the persuasive and imaginative tasks. Chapter 5 presents a summary of results for a number of demographic subgroups and for the impact of home factors on writing achievement.

Chapter

Informative Writing

Informative writing is used to share knowledge and convey messages, instructions, and ideas. It ranges from simple reports or retellings of what has happened to complex analyses and explanations. It can draw on the writer's previous knowledge and experience, or it can be based on new information that must be examined in order to complete the task successfully.

Skill in informative writing is necessary in day-to-day life, academic study, business, and the professions. At one level, informative writing includes writing letters, ordering items through the mail, and completing forms and job applications. At another level, it includes summaries and reports or instructions on how to do something new. At a still more complex level, informative writing includes explanations and analyses of why things work as they do or are as they are—the tracing of causes and effects, motivations for particular actions, or underlying foundations for opinions and points of view. These are the skills necessary for successful academic study and for understanding complex situations in business and the professions.

Informative writing tasks included in the 1984 assessment were chosen to reflect this diversity: Some tasks drew on writers' previous knowledge and experience; some provided new information (in words or pictures) as the basis for what was to be written; some asked for a simple report or description; some required drawing comparisons and contrasts; some asked for explanations. Formats also varied, including traditional school essays, letters, and news reports.

Of the eight informative writing tasks in the 1984 assessment, six required reports of information and two asked for analyses of information. Some exercises drew on the writers' previous knowledge, while others were based on information given as part of the task.

All writing samples were scored for their effectiveness in addressing the specific task that had been assigned. Responses were either rated as **unsatisfactory, minimal, adequate,** or **elaborated,** or they were **not rated.** (A general explanation of these levels is given in Chapter 1.)

Reporting from Personal Experience

Two items asked students for reports based on information drawn from the writers' own experiences. Brief paraphrases of the assignments are provided below.*

> Job Application: Provide a brief description of a desirable summer job and describe previous experiences or qualifications for such a job.

> Pets: Write a note explaining to a friend how to care for a pet while away on vacation, including where to find the food, how often to feed the pet, and how much food to give the pet.

Results for these two reporting tasks are given in **Table 2.1** and **Figure 2.1**. Across these simple tasks, the majority of students (73 to 89 percent) at all three grade levels wrote at least **minimal** responses; by grade 11, 65 percent were writing **adequate** responses.

For pets, 73 percent of the fourth graders wrote responses that were rated at least **minimal**, but only 2 percent provided **adequate** responses that included all of the information necessary to ensure that the pet would be fed properly.

Responses rated as **minimal** mentioned such things as food and water but took for granted that the friend would know how much or how frequently the pet should be fed or where the food was to be found. The following samples, reproduced verbatim, are typical:

> I would really appreciate it if you would take care of my dog while I'm gone. feed him and water him 1 time a day. The food is in the cabinet. let him loose every 2 days to get his exercise.

> Hi! Could I ask you a favor. Could you feed my pets for two weeks. Heres how you do it. Give the dogs a panful each of freesh water everyday. Mix the dog food with ware water. I would appreciate it. Thank you. Could you also keep an eye on them. the neighbors does always fight our dogs.

Such responses indicate that the writers clearly understood the task, even if they were careless about what they included or assumed the friend already knew what to do.

*The exact wording of these writing tasks and others cited in this report has not been published because some of them will be used in future assessments.

In any event, the writing that resulted was not in itself sufficient to ensure proper care of the pet.

By grade 8, the proportion of at least **minimal** papers had risen to 89 percent, and 19 percent included all of the necessary information about food and water for the pet.

Informative Writing—Reporting

TABLE 2.1

Percentage of Students at or Above the Minimal
and Adequate Levels of Task Accomplishment

WRITING TASK	GRADE 4		GRADE 8		GRADE 11	
From Personal Experience	% Minimal or Better	% Adequate or Better	% Minimal or Better	% Adequate or Better	% Minimal or Better	% Adequate or Better
Pets	73.2	2.1	89.1	18.9	—	—
Job Application	—	—	—	—	81.2	64.9
From Given Information						
Plants	85.4	41.2	—	—	—	—
Appleby House	68.2	24.1	86.8	52.4	86.5	59.4
XYZ Company	46.3	34.4	85.5	67.2	—	—
Dali	41.7	2.9	72.2	17.4	81.8	31.7

The second reporting task, involving a job application, was given only at grade 11. Ninety-two percent of the students were able to fill in requested information, such as birthdate, height, and weight. When asked to describe a desirable job and their qualifications for it, most (81 percent) provided at least **minimal** responses and 65 percent provided at least **adequate**, if not fully elaborated, descriptions. The following student samples illustrate the range of **adequate** responses:

TO WHOM IT MAY CONCERN

I would like a job helping to take care of the animals at the S.P.C.A. I love animals. I have experience with animals. I have two dogs, four birdss one hamster I had more animals but old age the have died. I love dog the best and I feel I could do the job.

I would like to work with children either in a day care center or in a hospital I have a seven year old sister and I babysit a lot, so I know al about children. Also, I took a course in first aid and a course in child care and Development.

Job preferably in a hospital or nursing home, working with charts, medication sheets and tickets. Working in a doctor's office as a receptionist, answering the telephone, keeping patients' charts.

Volunteer work in local nursing home, school and on-the-job training at hospital as a unit clerk-reseptionist.

Informative Writing—

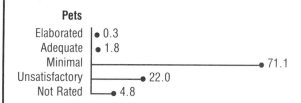

GRADE 4

From Personal Experience

Pets

Elaborated	0.3
Adequate	1.8
Minimal	71.1
Unsatisfactory	22.0
Not Rated	4.8

From Given Information

Plants

Adequate	41.2
Minimal	44.2
Unsatisfactory	12.6
Not Rated	2.0

Appleby House

Elaborated	0.6
Adequate	23.5
Minimal	44.1
Unsatisfactory	28.0
Not Rated	3.8

XYZ Company

Adequate	34.4
Minimal	11.9
Unsatisfactory	50.1
Not Rated	3.6

Dali

Elaborated	0.0
Adequate	2.8
Minimal	38.8
Unsatisfactory	49.8
Not Rated	8.5

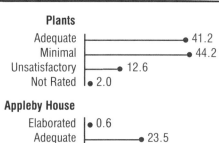
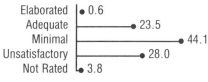
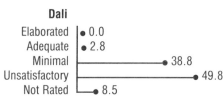

Reporting

Percentage of Students at Each Level of Task Accomplishment

FIGURE 2.1

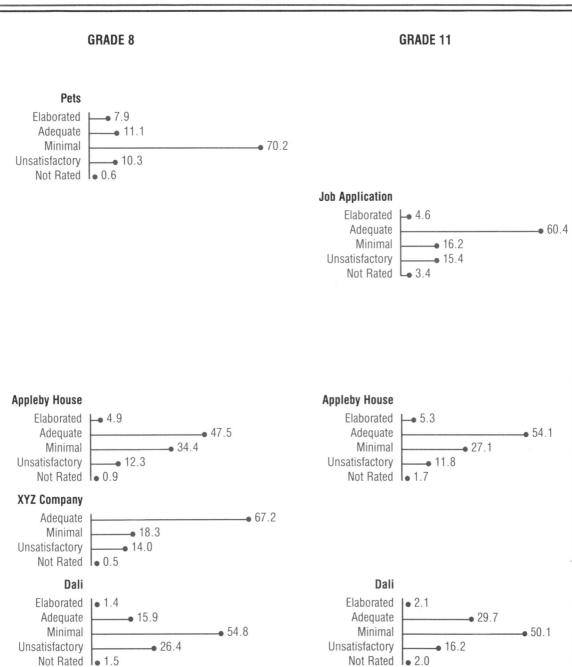

GRADE 8

GRADE 11

Pets

Elaborated	7.9
Adequate	11.1
Minimal	70.2
Unsatisfactory	10.3
Not Rated	0.6

Job Application

Elaborated	4.6
Adequate	60.4
Minimal	16.2
Unsatisfactory	15.4
Not Rated	3.4

Appleby House

Elaborated	4.9
Adequate	47.5
Minimal	34.4
Unsatisfactory	12.3
Not Rated	0.9

XYZ Company

Adequate	67.2
Minimal	18.3
Unsatisfactory	14.0
Not Rated	0.5

Dali

Elaborated	1.4
Adequate	15.9
Minimal	54.8
Unsatisfactory	26.4
Not Rated	1.5

Appleby House

Elaborated	5.3
Adequate	54.1
Minimal	27.1
Unsatisfactory	11.8
Not Rated	1.7

Dali

Elaborated	2.1
Adequate	29.7
Minimal	50.1
Unsatisfactory	16.2
Not Rated	2.0

A few students (about 5 percent for Job Application) went beyond **adequate** responses, providing coherent, appropriately **elaborated** accounts. The following is an example:

> Mainly, I would like to be a lifeguard, working at a neighorhood swimming pool. I would also like to help with swim lessons and if there is one, swim team.
>
> I have participated in swim clubs since I was 10 years old. I swam on the varsity swim team my sophmore year in school. I have also helped teach young children how to swim, mainly children I babysat in summer, and relatives.
>
> At the present, I am waiting for my life saving class to begin.

To summarize, almost all students at grade 4 wrote at least **minimal** reports in response to tasks that involved presenting information from personal experience. Performance on these tasks improved across the grades, so that by grade 11 nearly two-thirds of the students were writing at least **adequate** responses. Less than 8 percent of the students at any age, however, were able to provide **elaborated** responses.

Reporting from Given Information

Four of the reporting tasks asked students for descriptions of various types of information provided as part of the task itself.

> Plants: Summarize a science experiment depicted in a brief series of pictures showing different stages of a plant's growth.
>
> Appleby House: Write a newspaper article based on notes provided about an unusual haunted house.
>
> XYZ Company: Explain that a previously ordered T-shirt had not been received, and propose a course of action.
>
> Dali: Describe a surrealistic painting by Salvador Dali, shown on an accompanying card.

For reporting tasks based on given information, there were sharp differences in performance across the tasks administered at each grade level. (See Table 2.1 and Figure 2.1.) At grade 4, 85 percent of the students provided at least a **minimal** description of the pictured steps in the science experiment (Plants), and 41 percent of the descriptions were rated as **adequate.** Fourth graders also did fairly well explaining about the T-shirt and using the information provided to write about the haunted house, with many students writing **minimal** responses and 34 percent and 24 percent, respectively, writing **adequate** responses. In contrast, fewer than half (42 percent) provided even a **minimal** description of the painting by Dali, and only 3 percent of the responses were rated as **adequate.**

At grade 8, the great majority (72 to 87 percent) of responses on each of the tasks were rated as at least **minimal.** However, as with the fourth graders, the percentage of **adequate** responses varied considerably, from 17 percent for Dali to 52 percent and 67 percent, respectively, for the Appleby House and XYZ Company tasks. The majority of eighth graders were able to write **adequate** reports from given information, as long as that information was relatively straightforward. However, the task of describing a surrealistic painting was rather difficult.

Given the relatively good performance on the straightforward writing tasks at grade 8, improvements between grades 8 and 11 were modest. Even at grade 11, only 32 percent of the descriptions of the Dali painting were rated as **adequate.**

The Dali task was more difficult than the other reporting tasks because it required students to adopt a consistent strategy for organizing the details selected so that someone else could "see" the picture clearly. Most students simply enumerated details chosen from the picture or provided a running commentary that relied on the presence of the picture. Such responses were rated as **minimal:**

> This picture was a desert, with cliffs on the right side. There are three melting clocks. One of them is hanging on a tree branch, one is lying on a fossil (or bone), and the other is dropping down a box. The tree is planted in the box, and there is an unmelted clock on it. There is a mirror or sheet of glass on the sea shore. The cliffs are gold colored. The tree is dead.

To provide an **adequate** description of the picture, students had to relate the details one to another:

> In the background there is a lake or ocean with a yellowish brown cliff juting out of the still water. By the ocean there is a large blue platform. Another platform brown in color is close to you on the left side. On it ther is a orange pocket watch with black ants on it. Hanging of the edge there is a gold pocket watch with a fly on it, but the watch is melted so half of it is on the platform half is off. Right next to the gold watch there is a dead gray tree with a similer watch melting off it, but silver in color. In the midle of the picture is a melted face with a large eye (closed) with long eye lashes with a silver pocket watch melting off it.

In summary, students at all three grade levels were able to write **adequately** from given information for some tasks, but had difficulty with other tasks. Generally, the simpler and clearer the information provided, the more successful students were in summarizing and presenting it. More complex material required more complex writing strategies. Even at grade 11, some types of writing from given information remained difficult.

Analytic Writing

Informative writing also includes tasks that require students to analyze rather than simply present information. Analytic writing builds upon describing and reporting skills and also requires that writers explain relationships among the ideas and information they are dealing with. Analytic writing marks a shift from the simple *what* happened to a concern with *why* it happened as it did, from describing to explaining. Two analytic writing tasks were included in the assessment:

Favorite Music: Describe a favorite type of music and explain why it is liked.

Food on the Frontier: This task began with a passage about frontier life; students were asked to read the passage and then to compare modern-day food with frontier food.

Table 2.2 and **Figure 2.2** summarize results for these two tasks. At each grade level, the analytic tasks proved to be the most difficult of the items that asked for informative writing. At grade 4, just over half the students managed even **minimal** responses to one task and fewer than half on the second task; even at grade 11, fewer than one-fourth of the students managed **adequate** analyses.

For Favorite Music, about half the fourth graders (53 percent) and 80 to 81 percent of the eighth and eleventh graders were able to write at least **minimal** responses, selecting a favorite type of music and giving one or more brief reasons why they liked it. In papers rated as **minimal,** however, these reasons were strung together, rather than organized into a coherent explanation:

> I love Rock and Roll because it lets you get down itss not so boring. I love going to concerts.

> I like Thriller because it sound good and I like the way it start like someone making noise. And the beat sound good and I like the way man talk and it sound a ghost story.

> My favorite kind of music is slow pop or rock.

> I'm having some problems over friends and a ex-boyfriend and when I listen to pop it helps me figure out my problems. I don't like slow songs with all music. My favorite pop singer is Linoll Richard my favorite groups is "Airstepp". "Truly" and "Just Once" is my favorite songs.

Even in the upper grades, very few of the students (no more than 7 or 8 percent) were able to take this task a step further and provide an organized explanation of their preferences instead of a rambling commentary. The following example illustrates the relatively simple type of explanation that was necessary for a response to be rated as **adequately** accomplishing this task:

> My favorite kind of music is soft, easy rock because it is soothing and relaxing. I don't like the hard rock kind, it give me a headache. Soft rock has a nice beat, but it doesn't annoy you like hard rock. It's easy to sing along with, too, because you can understand what they're saying.

Food on the Frontier differed from Favorite Music in that the writing was based in part on information provided as part of the task; it also differed in that it asked for comparison and contrast between frontier food and modern-day food rather than for explanations for personal preferences. At grade 4, this task was slightly more difficult than Favorite Music: Only 40 percent (compared with 53 percent) managed at least **minimal** responses, and merely 2 percent provided **adequate** answers. By grade 11, however, 85 percent of the responses were at least **minimal,** and 25 percent were **adequate.**

In summary, fourth-grade students did very poorly on the analytic writing tasks, but by grade 8 the majority of students provided responses indicating at least a **minimal** understanding of what such tasks required. Even at grade 11, however, fewer than one-fourth of the students were able to write **adequate** responses to such tasks.

Informative Writing—Analytic

TABLE 2.2

Percentage of Students at or Above the Minimal
and Adequate Levels of Task Accomplishment

	GRADE 4		GRADE 8		GRADE 11	
From Personal Information	% Minimal or Better	% Adequate or Better	% Minimal or Better	% Adequate or Better	% Minimal or Better	% Adequate or Better
Favorite Music	52.9	1.9	80.3	8.3	80.9	7.0
From Given Information						
Food on the Frontier	40.3	1.9	81.0	18.3	85.2	24.6

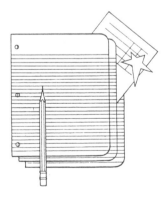

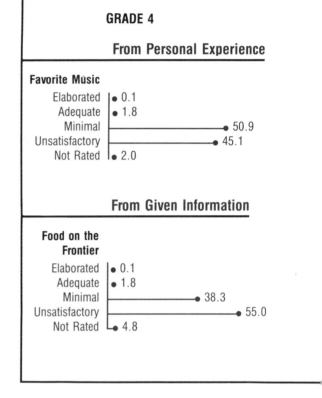

Informative Writing—

GRADE 4

From Personal Experience

Favorite Music

Elaborated	0.1
Adequate	1.8
Minimal	50.9
Unsatisfactory	45.1
Not Rated	2.0

From Given Information

Food on the Frontier

Elaborated	0.1
Adequate	1.8
Minimal	38.3
Unsatisfactory	55.0
Not Rated	4.8

Summary: Informative Writing

How well can American students complete informative writing tasks? Clearly, the answer to this question depends on the particular writing task. By grade 11, 59 to 65 percent wrote **adequate** descriptions based on familiar, relatively simple information or experiences; only 32 percent, however, wrote an **adequate** description of a modern painting. Informative writing that required analysis, whether of one's own preferences or of similarities and differences based on a social science passage, was much more difficult. While 80 percent or more of the students provided at least **minimal** responses (recognizing the basic elements that go into an analytic writing task), even at grade 11 only 7 to 25 percent provided **adequate** responses to these tasks.

The poor performance on the analytic tasks is particularly disturbing in that success on such tasks is a prerequisite for academic success. These are the tasks that reflect the ability to provide evidence, reason logically, and make a well-developed point. They

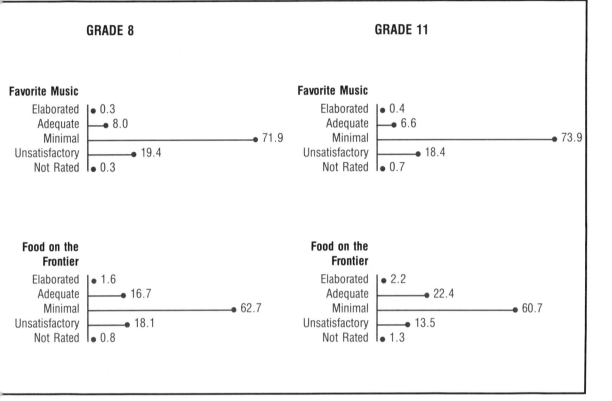

Analytic

FIGURE 2.2

Percentage of Students at Each Level of Task Accomplishment

GRADE 8

Favorite Music

Elaborated	0.3
Adequate	8.0
Minimal	71.9
Unsatisfactory	19.4
Not Rated	0.3

Food on the Frontier

Elaborated	1.6
Adequate	16.7
Minimal	62.7
Unsatisfactory	18.1
Not Rated	0.8

GRADE 11

Favorite Music

Elaborated	0.4
Adequate	6.6
Minimal	73.9
Unsatisfactory	18.4
Not Rated	0.7

Food on the Frontier

Elaborated	2.2
Adequate	22.4
Minimal	60.7
Unsatisfactory	13.5
Not Rated	1.3

reflect the "reasoned and disciplined thinking" called for in earlier assessment reports[*] and the "skilled intelligence" extolled by the Commission on Excellence in Education.[**]

Before discussing these results further, however, we should consider performance on the persuasive writing tasks discussed in the next chapter. These tasks require similar types of argument and analysis.

[*]*Reading, Thinking and Writing, Results from the 1979–80 National Assessment of Reading and Literature.* Education Commission of the States, 1981.

[**] *A Nation at Risk: The Imperative for Educational Reform.* The National Commission on Excellence in Education, 1983.

Chapter

Persuasive Writing

Persuasive writing communicates specific points of view in order to influence others and bring about some kind of change. People use it to offer advice they hope will be taken, to win advocates for their points of view, to defend their opinions or positions, or to argue for a particular course of action.

Persuasive writing can range from highly formal to highly informal—from a chatty letter urging a friend to visit to a political treatise calling for governmental reform. It can include emotional appeals and logical arguments, each in its appropriate place and proportion.

In all types of persuasive writing, the writer must take a point of view and support it. Sometimes opposing points of view are known and confronted; at other times personal opinions are simply promulgated. In addition to knowledge of the topic, persuasive writing requires an awareness of audience and of ways to influence others. Persuasive writing permeates our society and is one of the marks of an involved social or academic thinker.

The persuasive writing tasks included in the assessment were of two types: those that asked students to convince others to adopt a point of view and those that required students to refute an opposing point of view.

Writing to Convince Others to Adopt Your Point of View

One set of persuasive writing tasks presented the students with a problematic situation and asked them to state their opinion and explain or support it with reasons or an argument. Some exercises offered possible courses of action and others required the students to respond based on their personal experience and knowledge. In each case, the writers needed to be responsive to the implicit concerns of the audience to whom they were writing.

> Spaceship: Decide whether creatures from another planet should be allowed to return home or be detained for scientific study, and convince others of this point of view.
>
> Dissecting Frogs: Discuss and support views on dissecting frogs in science class.
>
> Space Program: Take a stand on whether funding for the space program should be cut and explain why.
>
> Split Session: Write a letter to the principal defending a request for a morning or afternoon school session.
>
> Swimming Pool: Write a convincing letter to get a summer job helping out at a swimming pool.
>
> School Rule: Select a school rule and convince the principal that it needs changing.

Table 3.1 and Figure 3.1 show the results for these writing tasks. A substantially smaller percentage of students at all three grades wrote at the **adequate** level than wrote at the **minimal** level. Between 53 percent (Swimming Pool) and 67 percent (Spaceship) of the fourth graders were able to complete the three tasks administered to their age group at least at the **minimal** level, but only between 4 percent (School Rule) and 24 percent (Spaceship) completed the same tasks at least at the **adequate** level. Similar patterns—substantially smaller percentages displaying **adequate** performance—were reflected in the results for eighth and eleventh graders. While the students were able to understand the assignment and to present a point of view, they generally were unable to support their ideas beyond general statements and personal likes and dislikes.

School rule is a case in point. This task asked the students to write a letter to their principal, naming a rule that they felt should be changed and explaining why the school did not need that rule. The majority of students at all three grade levels (58 percent of the fourth graders, 69 percent of the eighth graders, and 69 percent of the eleventh graders) were able to name a rule and indicate that it should be dropped or changed, but their reasons tended to revolve around their own individual wishes, instead of being reasoned arguments that would appeal to a principal. Far fewer students (4 percent of the fourth graders, 15 percent of the eighth graders, and 22 percent of the eleventh graders) wrote **adequately** supported letters in which they gave at least one appropriate reason for their choice beyond "It's not fair" or purely emotional outbursts on matters of personal inconvenience and preference. (Such outbursts, while reflecting the students' feelings, are unlikely to have the desired persuasive effect.)

The following response, for example, received an **unsatisfactory** rating because the writer's views were not supported at all.

> That we should be able to horseplay in the court yard at lunch. To run and play at lunch time.

TABLE 3.1

Persuasive Writing—Convincing Others

**Percentage of Students at or Above the Minimal
and Adequate Levels of Task Accomplishment**

	GRADE 4		GRADE 8		GRADE 11	
	% Minimal or Better	% Adequate or Better	% Minimal or Better	% Adequate or Better	% Minimal or Better	% Adequate or Better
School Rule	61.7	4.1	83.5	14.6	90.1	21.7
Dissecting Frogs	—	—	84.8	17.9	—	—
Swimming Pool	53.3	4.5	66.7	12.0	75.9	19.4
Split Sessions	—	—	34.4	9.0	59.8	15.1
Spaceship	66.8	23.5	—	—	—	—
Space Program	—	—	—	—	82.0	28.0

Thirty-six percent of the fourth graders, 16 percent of the eighth graders, and 9 percent of the eleventh graders wrote **unsatisfactory** responses, reflecting their inability to provide any reasons or discussion in support of their points of view.

Most of the students at each grade level wrote letters of a quality similar to this one:

> I Think our school does not need A labotory rule because some time people have to go and they would let you and then when your doing your work one of the teachers happen to get up and mosy on out to the restroom to go to the bathroom just after she or he told you your not alound to go to the rest room.
> another rule I dont like is the Cafeteria rule that iF their is something under your Feet you have to pick it up and I think that is sick because sometime that stuFF is not yours and its been stepped on are oFF oF and then Mr. Russel walks over and tell you to go through it away And iF you reFuss he makes you sit st the penlty table.

While this paper involved much more writing, it received a **minimal** rating because, although the reasons given for changing the rules are highly personal reflections of the author's experiences, they are hardly appropriate to seeing the change as beneficial to the school in general and for moving the principal to action. Additionally, while the principal may not necessarily be opposed to change, there was probably an initial reason for the institution of the rule. Some explanation about why that reason is no longer relevant or an alternative way to address the concern might be necessary to convince the principal.

Far fewer students wrote at the **adequate** level, with fewer than one-fifth of them providing reasons having a wider application or suggesting and supporting a new or revised rule. An example of such supporting discussion is found in the paper below:

> I don't think the rule for students to stay at the dances instead of coming and going as they please is necessary. If the question that perhaps the students will leave, become intoxicated, and return comes into your mind just have the policeman that chaperones our dances to pay attention to incoming students. This rule makes coming and going for medical reasons, forgetting something or someone, or going to buy somethin to eat difficult if not impossible. I understand that the school is responsible for us if we become injured on school grounds but if we leave what difference is it to you.
>
> I suggest a pass should be handed out upon the payment on arrival, at the dance and on the comings and goings of the passes' owner it should be stamped.
>
> Thank you for your co-operation.
>
> sincerely,

Elaborated letters were rare, occurring less than 3 percent of the time for eleventh graders and less than 1 percent of the time for fourth and eighth graders. Papers receiving this rating provided a well-organized series of examples or an argument or both, with reasons having a wider application:

> I am writing this letter in order to discuss the rule of "sharing lockers". I know I don't like this rule and I'm sure many other peple don't like it either. I think I can understand why you would like lockers to be shared. I guess the first reason would be so that new kids to the school can have an almost "automatic friend". Another reason could be a shortage of lockers.
>
> I believe this rule should be abolished because I know about myself and others who had books "borrowed" without permission. This causes trouble when one is forced to go to class without his books. My locker partner also smokes, which is a severe problem. Our locker always smells of smoke. The locker shortage can be solved by placing a row or two of lockers in the basement.
>
> Thank you very much for taking your time to read this and I hope you will give it some thought.
>
> Sincerely,

GRADE 4

School Rule

Elaborated	0.2
Adequate	3.9
Minimal	57.6
Unsatisfactory	36.1
Not Rated	2.2

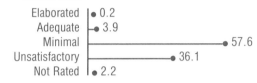

Swimming Pool

Elaborated	0.2
Adequate	4.3
Minimal	48.8
Unsatisfactory	40.2
Not Rated	6.5

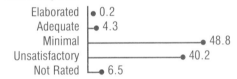

Spaceship

Elaborated	0.7
Adequate	22.8
Minimal	43.3
Unsatisfactory	26.8
Not Rated	6.4

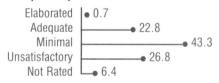

FIGURE 3.1

Convincing Others
Percentage of Students at Each Level
of Task Accomplishment

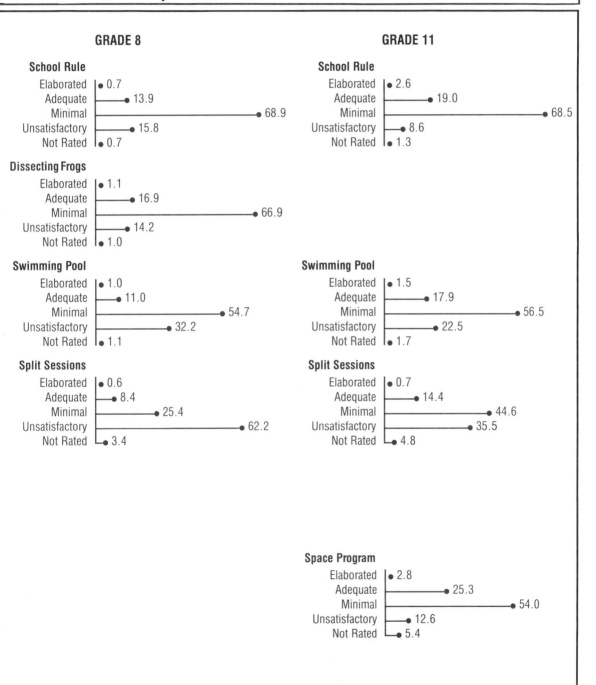

GRADE 8

School Rule
- Elaborated • 0.7
- Adequate • 13.9
- Minimal • 68.9
- Unsatisfactory • 15.8
- Not Rated • 0.7

Dissecting Frogs
- Elaborated • 1.1
- Adequate • 16.9
- Minimal • 66.9
- Unsatisfactory • 14.2
- Not Rated • 1.0

Swimming Pool
- Elaborated • 1.0
- Adequate • 11.0
- Minimal • 54.7
- Unsatisfactory • 32.2
- Not Rated • 1.1

Split Sessions
- Elaborated • 0.6
- Adequate • 8.4
- Minimal • 25.4
- Unsatisfactory • 62.2
- Not Rated • 3.4

GRADE 11

School Rule
- Elaborated • 2.6
- Adequate • 19.0
- Minimal • 68.5
- Unsatisfactory • 8.6
- Not Rated • 1.3

Swimming Pool
- Elaborated • 1.5
- Adequate • 17.9
- Minimal • 56.5
- Unsatisfactory • 22.5
- Not Rated • 1.7

Split Sessions
- Elaborated • 0.7
- Adequate • 14.4
- Minimal • 44.6
- Unsatisfactory • 35.5
- Not Rated • 4.8

Space Program
- Elaborated • 2.8
- Adequate • 25.3
- Minimal • 54.0
- Unsatisfactory • 12.6
- Not Rated • 5.4

31

Writing to Refute an Opposing Point of View

Some of the persuasive tasks required the students to take a stand and to argue their position against an opposing view. To complete these tasks, the students needed to be responsive to the opposition. The exercises in this category were as follows:

Aunt May: Write a letter convincing Aunt May it is alright to travel alone even though Aunt May thinks otherwise.

Radio Station: Give reasons why the class should be allowed to visit a local radio station despite the manager's concerns.

Recreation Opportunities: Take a stand on whether a railroad track or a warehouse should be purchased. Using arguments based on possible recreational opportunities, defend this choice and refute the alternative.

Uncle: Write a letter refuting an uncle's concerns about lending his car to visit a friend.

Bike Lane: Take a stand on whether a bike lane should be installed and refute the opposing view.

The results for these tasks are shown in **Table 3.2** and **Figure 3.2.** Far more students wrote at the **minimal** than at the **adequate** levels. Twenty-three to 30 percent of the fourth graders, 33 to 38 percent of the eighth graders, and 39 to 50 percent of the eleventh graders stated their point of view and provided brief support. However, only between 14 and 34 percent provided **adequate** support.

For example, Radio Station asked students to write a letter to a station manager who did not want a class to visit because his recording studio was too small and the class would make too much noise. The letter needed to convince the manager to change his mind. Forty-seven percent of the fourth graders and 28 percent of the eighth graders wrote **unsatisfactory** papers, reflecting their inability to write a letter that even alluded to the concerns of their audience. While responses at this level focused on the visit to a radio station, they did not try to change the manager's mind and tended to beg rather than argue with the manager. The following is an example of such a letter:

> Dear Mr. Station Manager:
> Me and my class would really like to visit your studio. We are all concerned about it. We were hoping you could change your mind. We would love to go and see all the equiptment.
> Thank
> You.
> Sincerely,

About one-third of the students wrote **minimal** letters, reflecting their inability to focus on their audience and to go beyond superficially answering the manager's concerns. The following paper addresses the manager's concern about noise, but not his concern about space. Thirty percent of the fourth graders and 38 percent of the eighth graders wrote refutations at this level.

Persuasive Writing—Refuting an Opposing Position

TABLE 3.2

Percentage of Students at or Above the Minimal
and Adequate Levels of Task Accomplishment

	GRADE 4		GRADE 8		GRADE 11	
	% Minimal or Better	% Adequate or Better	% Minimal or Better	% Adequate or Better	% Minimal or Better	% Adequate or Better
Recreation Opportunity	—	—	47.3	14.3	71.1	24.6
Radio Station	46.6	16.2	71.0	33.5	—	—
Aunt May	48.6	25.2	—	—	—	—
Uncle	—	—	—	—	73.6	24.1
Bike Lane	—	—	—	—	66.0	26.9

Dear Mr. Smithfield:
   Our class is among the mst mature in Lake Braddock. We have gone on many field trips before and I assure you we are very quiet and respect others rights. We would be very grateful and would have an excellent learning experience if you let us visit at some conveinient time.
   Thank you for your consideration.
      Signature

Only 16 percent of the fourth graders and 34 percent of the eighth graders, however, wrote letters of refutation rated as **adequate** or better. Almost none of them (4 percent of the eighth graders and less than 1 percent of the fourth graders) wrote **elaborated** papers providing reasons explicitly responsive to the manager's concerns. Since evaluations focused on content rather than mechanics, the following response was rated **adequate,** even though it contains errors in writing mechanics:

Dear Mr. Brown:
   Our class has suggested to have a field trip to your studio. We have been studying about radios and radio waves. We would like to be shown these methods on how they are done. We have decided to pay our own way to go there. We also

Persuasive Writing—

GRADE 4

Radio Station

Elaborated	0.4
Adequate	15.8
Minimal	30.4
Unsatisfactory	47.1
Not Rated	6.3

Aunt May

Elaborated	1.9
Adequate	23.3
Minimal	23.4
Unsatisfactory	44.5
Not Rated	6.9

FIGURE 3.2

Refuting an Opposing Position

Percentage of Students at Each Level
of Task Accomplishment

GRADE 8

**Recreation
Opportunity**

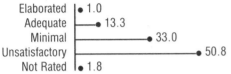

Elaborated ● 1.0
Adequate ● 13.3
Minimal ● 33.0
Unsatisfactory ● 50.8
Not Rated ● 1.8

Radio Station

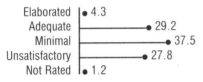

Elaborated ● 4.3
Adequate ● 29.2
Minimal ● 37.5
Unsatisfactory ● 27.8
Not Rated ● 1.2

GRADE 11

**Recreation
Opportunity**

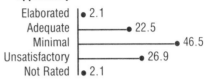

Elaborated ● 2.1
Adequate ● 22.5
Minimal ● 46.5
Unsatisfactory ● 26.9
Not Rated ● 2.1

Bike Lane

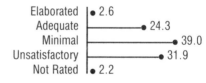

Elaborated ● 2.6
Adequate ● 24.3
Minimal ● 39.0
Unsatisfactory ● 31.9
Not Rated ● 2.2

Uncle

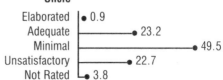

Elaborated ● 0.9
Adequate ● 23.2
Minimal ● 49.5
Unsatisfactory ● 22.7
Not Rated ● 3.8

made a solem promise to be quiet. We are going to break down in groups and each group will go one at a time. Please think this over and I am grateful that you shall put some thought into this.

Our class have solved your problem and I hope you will put some thought into this. I myself would like to go in and discover the radio programs. Sone of our students have their future as a radio programer. Thank you for you consideration.

Sincley,

The eleventh graders' responses to these tasks followed a similar pattern. On the Recreational Opportunity task, the eleventh graders did much better than the eighth graders: 71 percent were rated **minimal** or better (compared with 47 percent at grade 8). But even at grade 11, only 24 to 27 percent of the responses to the three tasks were rated **adequate** or better.

Summary: Persuasive Writing

Results of student performance on persuasive writing tasks are dismaying. Across 11 tasks of varying difficulty, between 9 and 36 percent of the eleventh-grade students wrote **unsatisfactory** responses and less than 3 percent wrote **elaborated** responses. While the majority of students wrote persuasively at the **minimal** level or better, fewer than one-third could do so at the **adequate** level or better. The students at grade 4 also performed poorly on these tasks, between 27 and 47 percent writing **unsatisfactory** papers and fewer than 2 percent writing **elaborated** papers.

The low percentage of **adequate** responses gives cause for concern, as does the high percentage of **unsatisfactory** papers. Although persuasive writing might seem to be difficult, it requires the kind of arguing children also need when they want to "have their way" in their daily lives. It is also the kind of writing they are likely to need as adults in their personal and work experiences. Even though situations involving persuasion are common for students, results of this assessment indicate that students' persuasive writing skills are not well developed. Perhaps this reflects a lack of practice in persuasive writing across the school years.

Chapter

Imaginative Writing

The third broad area of the 1984 assessment dealt with imaginative writing, which includes the entire range of literary and expressive writing. Such tasks may ask writers to tell personal or fictional stories or to project themselves into a situation and elaborate upon the feelings or atmosphere that the situation evokes. Imaginative writing shapes and expresses the thoughts and feelings of writers; in its more structured forms, it can evolve into traditional literary genres such as stories, poems, plays, or song lyrics. Three imaginative writing tasks were included in the 1984 assessment:

> Hole in the Box: Given a picture of a box with a hole in it and an eye peeking out, imagine being in the picture. describe the scene and how it feels to be part of it.

> Ghost Story: Write a good, scary ghost story.

> Flashlight: Write a story about adventures with a flashlight with special powers.

Results for these three tasks are displayed in **Table 4.1** and **Figure 4.1**

For the two tasks that asked for stories, Ghost Story and Flashlight, most of the students at all three grade levels were able to write at least at the **minimal** level. Almost all the eighth and eleventh graders (88 to 90 percent) managed **minimal** stories. At fourth grade, 81 percent wrote **minimal** or better ghost stories, and two-thirds wrote at least **minimal** adventure stories in response to the Flashlight task. Responses at the **minimal** level attempted the basic task of storytelling, but did not develop the stories successfully. Sometimes students provided only the bare outlines of a plot, with little or no elaboration of detail; sometimes they rambled, providing a catalog of events without a point or structure; sometimes they began to tell a story, but never got further than the beginning. The following examples illustrate the range of responses at the **minimal** level:

One Saturday night. It was raining and it was dark out, are car went off the rode. We walk about 78 mmiles. We got to a house, wew knocked on the door. A man answer it, he was ugly. We asked if we could use his phone. We walked in. When we tuirned around he was gone. We saw the phone we ran to it, it was dead, We heard the door slam and lock. We ran to the door and the man started floating up. Sudenly he fadded away the lock broke and the door swung open it was daylight. That why we disapered. We ran to our car and walked to the gastation and they towed us to town.
The END

I took the flashlight turned it on and used it to make me powerful. I became the President of the United States for a while just to get the feel of it. Then I made a mantion and lived in it till my time ran out.

I would turn the flashlight on and get me a new car. Then I would come to school and go a change my grades with it. Then I would get all the money I could with it.

I took the flashlight turned on and then this genie appeared be for by eyes and said he was mine for twenty four hours so I told him I wanted my teeth straitend out, to clean my room & to give me 1 million dollars and he said my wish was granted. Hee snaped his fingers & everything was done & he handed me a suitcase with 1 million dollars sin it & said it was mine to keep. That night me & my whole family & genie all flew to Paris franse also got to stay in a palace it was georgeous the genie left the next day while we toured Europe & thge world. When we got home our house was three stories high with everything ytou always wanted on it like an elevator rec. room two spas, two pods almost like Hearst castle, tennis coursts a new wardrobe for everybody. The house was filed with love & joy. My room had a trundle bed, bay windows, a balcony, a cordless phone everything I wanted. My parents bedrom had a king size bed, hugh closets fixed with clothes & a bathtub spa.

In contrast to these **minimal** attempts, some of the students were able to write **adequate** stories, with clear evidence of the storyteller's obligation to structure a plot and provide it with appropriate details. At grade 4, only 8 to 9 percent of the students managed **adequate** stories, but this rose sharply for both tasks by grade 8 (to 31 and 38 percent) and still more by grade 11 (36 percent for Flashlight, 48 percent for Ghost Story). At all three grades, Flashlight was somewhat more difficult than Ghost Story, primarily because of the temptation to let the Flashlight story degenerate into an unstructured wish list. The following examples represent stories rated as **adequate:**

I turned on this flashlight and I suddenly appeared in a different world in this world the grass was blue and the trees bright red. I walked on and I stumbled into a cave then wene I reached about halfway there a syclipse attacked me. I ran ferther and ferther into the cave but the syclipse was gaining on me. I realized that I had to do something so I turned on my flashlight and it turned into a giagantic (but light) sword. I swund at the monster and choped of his head. I walked for one hour before leaving the cave but whenb I left I was at a waterfront with a nine-hounddred man army I joined.

After about 2 mounths we were under a little vacation. My friend and I decided to go swimming and we went. One thing about this water was that you could breath under water so my friend Rob & I went really deep. about 5 minutees later we felt the ground shake we swam upward to see what it was. When we reached the top of the water the whole army was disdroyed. I fanted and the next thing I know I was home laying in bed.
THE END

In a far away land, where the tree's are always blowing and the lightening caracking there was a town which had been deserted for years. A young explorer named Alllen Pernor heard about the town and the mystery of the people that keep missing from the town. Allen set out with two friends name Fred and Ralph.

They took a van that was filled with machines that tookk pictures of ghosts and any sort of disturbances.

They went to the two to find a old man still living in the hotel. He rented them three rooms and reminded them of the mystery of missing people.

It was dark so they all went to bed. In the morning Fred and Ralph had disappered so Allen knew he was on his own.

There was a moor near the town. Allen went to check it out. When he got there he pick up a disturbance with one of his machines. He looked to the right of him and seen a ghost. He recorded on a tape recorder what he saw. The ghost grabbed him and he dropped the tape recorder.

The old man heard a scream and went to check it out. He saw a big bush moving he went toward it and as he look behind it something grabbed him and he was never seen again. Nothing was ever found no body, not even the tape recorder.

Imaginative Writing

TABLE 4.1

Percentage of Students at or Above the Minimal and Adequate Levels of Task Accomplishment

	GRADE 4		GRADE 8		GRADE 11	
	% Minimal or Better	% Adequate or Better	% Minimal or Better	% Adequate or Better	% Minimal or Better	% Adequate or Better
Hole in the Box	39.4	3.2	62.3	18.1	66.0	17.9
Flashlight	66.9	8.9	88.4	30.8	90.4	36.2
Ghost Story	81.4	8.2	88.9	37.5	88.3	48.3

GRADE 4

Hole in the Box

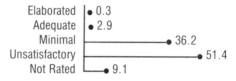

Elaborated	0.3
Adequate	2.9
Minimal	36.2
Unsatisfactory	51.4
Not Rated	9.1

Flashlight

Elaborated	0.2
Adequate	8.7
Minimal	58.0
Unsatisfactory	31.4
Not Rated	1.7

Ghost Story

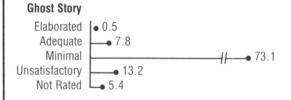

Elaborated	0.5
Adequate	7.8
Minimal	73.1
Unsatisfactory	13.2
Not Rated	5.4

Imaginative Writing
Percentage of Students at Each Level of Task Accomplishment

FIGURE 4.1

GRADE 8

Hole in the Box

Elaborated	3.5
Adequate	14.6
Minimal	44.2
Unsatisfactory	31.1
Not Rated	6.6

Flashlight

Elaborated	3.5
Adequate	27.3
Minimal	57.6
Unsatisfactory	11.3
Not Rated	0.3

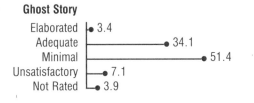

Ghost Story

Elaborated	3.4
Adequate	34.1
Minimal	51.4
Unsatisfactory	7.1
Not Rated	3.9

GRADE 11

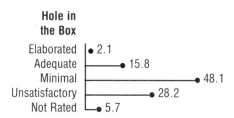

Hole in the Box

Elaborated	2.1
Adequate	15.8
Minimal	48.1
Unsatisfactory	28.2
Not Rated	5.7

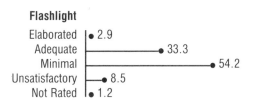

Flashlight

Elaborated	2.9
Adequate	33.3
Minimal	54.2
Unsatisfactory	8.5
Not Rated	1.2

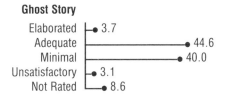

Ghost Story

Elaborated	3.7
Adequate	44.6
Minimal	40.0
Unsatisfactory	3.1
Not Rated	8.6

The third imaginative writing task, Hole in the Box, asked for a different set of writing skills. Rather than a story, it required imaginative projection into the scene and a discussion of the mood and activity surrounding the box. This was noticeably more difficult than the story tasks at all three grade levels. At grade 4, only 39 percent managed a **minimal** response or better. This rose to 62 percent at grade 8. Even at grade 11 only about two-thirds of the students managed even a **minimal** response such as the following:

> I want to get out but I can't. I'm not, hungry, & tierd. How soon I ask? People staring, yelling, screaming, & talking. People look at you thinking well he deserves it. Evil eyes looks at me, etc..Also no one I know is there it's like I'm in a magic place with no one to tell me it's okay. Every hole is to small to climb through.

Adequate responses were rare. They increased from 3 percent at grade 4 to 18 percent at grade 8. Even at grade 11, only 18 percent provided **adequate** responses, such as:

> I am trapped! I am stuck in a wooden box with geometrical shapes cut in it for air. Kids outside are playing games, running around, and eating. I am stuck! Maybe if I would have been nicer to everyone they wouldn't have stuck me in here. I wasn't good and now I'm stuck in a box on the grass. Next time I will be better. I never want to look at this box again! After my hour of staying in this tiny box is over I'll burn it. Yes, I'll burn it.

Summary: Imaginative Writing

By grade 4, two-thirds or more of the students understood the basic requirements of story writing and displayed at least **minimal** storytelling skills in response to story tasks. Although few of the fourth-grade students wrote fully **adequate** stories, these skills showed continued improvement at grade 8 and relatively modest additional improvement at grade 11.

When the students could not rely upon story frameworks, however, their imaginative writing was less successful. Even at grade 11, only 18 percent wrote **adequate** responses to the task requiring them to project themselves imaginatively into a scene and to provide a lively and interesting description of what was going on around them. Although eighth graders did better on this task than did fourth graders (18 percent **adequate** responses compared to 3 percent), there was no improvement between grade 8 and grade 11.

If we think of imaginative writing as a skill young children come to school with, as they spin imaginary stories to accompany their colorful scribbles, the results of this portion of the assessment are disappointing. While students at all three grade levels seem to have acquired some imaginative writing skills, these do not appear to become more varied across the school years. Perhaps because story writing is a skill young children already have to some degree, it is a kind of writing that schools neglect, particularly after the early elementary school years.

Chapter

Writing Performance Among Selected Subgroups

The data reported in the previous chapters illustrate the development of students' writing skills in response to particular tasks. In order to relate writing achievement to a number of student background characteristics in a way that permits comparisons across grade levels, NAEP used a new measurement technique called the Average Response Method (ARM) to estimate how well the students would have done if they had all taken all 10 informative and persuasive writing tasks administered to the eighth graders. (These tasks were presented and discussed in Chapters 2 and 3.)*

This measure of average writing achievement summarizes performance on a common scale that ranges from 0 to 400. The ARM measure of writing achievement is

*The ARM measure was limited to the results of these tasks because they were the only ones that could be linked, given the particular sampling design of this assessment.

based on the rating scale described in the preceding chapters, with a performance of all **not rated** responses equivalent to 0, an average of **unsatisfactory** responses equivalent to 100, an average of **minimal** responses equivalent to 200, an average of **adequate** responses equivalent to 300, and all **elaborated** responses being 400. (The Procedural Appendix contains further details about ARM scaling.)

Because of the comparability of results across grade levels, the ARM measure of average writing achievement will be used in this chapter* to compare achievement among various subgroups defined by demographic variables and home background factors. In later chapters, the same averages will be used to relate writing achievement to characteristics of instruction, students' writing practices, and students' attitudes toward and approaches to writing.

National Results

The average results for the nation on the 0-400 ARM scale are presented in **Table 5.1.**

National Average Writing Achievement (ARM)**

TABLE 5.1

GRADES	NATION
4	158 (1)
8	205 (1)
11	219 (1)

The national means, displayed in Table 5.1, show significant improvement in performance from grade 4 to grade 8 and continued (though less dramatic) improvement from grade 8 to grade 11. The less dramatic improvement from eighth to eleventh grade in part reflects the fact that from fourth to eighth grade represents a four-year interval, whereas from eighth to eleventh grade represents only a three-year

*There are some slight differences between computed results using ARM scaling procedures and straightforward averages of student performance across the samples who were given each writing task at each grade level. The results (and their standard errors) using both computational methods are presented in full in the Procedural Appendix, but briefly there are two basic differences. First, students at each grade level were administered a somewhat different set of tasks more appropriate for their abilities. Thus, fourth graders had an easier set of tasks than eighth graders, and eleventh graders had the most difficult set. Because of this, straightforward averages tend to be very similar across the grade levels and do not reflect improvements from grade level to grade level. In contrast, the ARM estimates how students at all three grades would perform on a common set of items; thus it provides information about improvement from grade level to grade level. Second, since the ARM scaling method is based on regression techniques, the results reflect some regression toward the mean, or shrinkage. At a given grade level the differences in performance for various groups reported in this and subsequent chapters will tend to be understated.

**Standard errors are presented in parentheses. It can be said with 95 percent certainty that the average writing achievement of the population of interest is in the interval of the estimated average ± 2 standard errors.

44

interval. Also, if we recall the item-by-item results in the previous chapters, the growth between grades 4 and 8 reflects in large part students' increasing ability to reach at least a solid **minimal** level of performance, while changes between grades 8 and 11 reflect students' generally slower progress toward **adequate** performance. It may be more difficult to move students beyond basic levels of performance than it is to teach them the fundamentals of written English, or it may be that instruction has emphasized basic performance to the detriment of more varied uses of written English.

Performance by Race/Ethnicity

Figure 5.1 presents the ARM results comparing the average writing achievement of Black, Hispanic, Asian-American, and White students at all three grade levels.

The results in Figure 5.1 suggest two major findings. First, at all three grades, Black and Hispanic students perform at substantially lower levels than do White and Asian-American students. Indeed, the writing achievement of eleventh-grade Black and

FIGURE 5.1

Average Writing Achievement (ARM)
for Black, Hispanic, Asian-American, and White Students

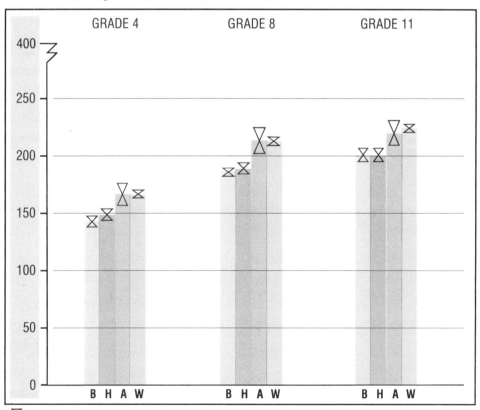

$\Huge\boxtimes$ = estimated average writing achievement and 95 percent confidence interval. It can be said with 95 percent certainty that the average writing achievement of the population of interest is in this interval.

THE NATION'S REPORT CARD

45

Hispanic students (200 points for both groups) is below that of eighth-grade White students (211 points). Second, grade-to-grade improvements in performance are relatively parallel for all four racial/ethnic groups. At grade 4, Black students' performance is 25 points below that of White students, and this difference remains essentially the same at grades 8 and 11 (25 points and 24 points, respectively). Hispanic students at grade 4 average 17 points below White students; this deficit increases substantially to 24 points at grade 8 and then remains constant from grade 8 to grade 11.

These seemingly parallel trends, however, may be deceptive. There are differences in dropout rates, with those for Black and particularly for Hispanic students being higher than those for White students.* If these dropouts had remained in school, the reported writing achievement of minority students at the upper grades would likely have been even lower than indicated here.

Asian-American students also participated in the assessment, but because so few were sampled at each grade level, the results of their performance must be interpreted with caution. It appears, however, that the performance of Asian-American students at all three grade levels is approximately equal to that of White students.

Performance of Other Demographic Subgroups

The assessment is designed to allow comparisons of performance among subgroups defined by a variety of other demographic variables, including sex, region of the country, and size and type of community. Average writing achievement levels for these groups are provided in **Table 5.2.** Writing achievement was significantly higher for females than for males and for students from advantaged-urban communities as compared to students from disadvantaged-urban or rural communities. Although achievement for students from the Northeast and Central regions tended to be slightly above that of students from the Southeastern and Western regions, differences in regional performance were negligible.**

As with the results for minority groups, patterns for other demographic subgroups suggest that achievement differences remain constant across grades. At grade 4, for example, achievement scores for students from disadvantaged-urban communities averaged 28 points below those from advantaged-urban communities. This difference remained essentially constant at grades 8 and 11 (averaging 33 and 27 points).

*Data from the National Longitudinal Surveys of Labor Market Experience show that dropout rates among youth age 18 during the period 1979-82 were 15 percent for White, 17 percent for Black, and 31 percent for Hispanic students. *School Dropouts*, United States General Accounting Office, June 1986.

**Regional results computed using straightforward averages differ slightly. See Procedural Appendix.

Average Writing Achievement (ARM)* for Demographic Subgroups

TABLE 5.2

SUBGROUPS	GRADES		
	4	8	11
Race/Ethnicity			
Black	138 (2)	186 (1)	200 (2)
Hispanic	146 (2)	188 (2)	200 (2)
Asian-American	163 (4)	211 (4)	219 (4)
White	163 (1)	211 (1)	224 (1)
Sex			
Male	150 (1)	196 (1)	209 (1)
Female	166 (1)	214 (1)	229 (1)
Region			
Northeast	161 (2)	209 (1)	222 (3)
Southeast	154 (2)	203 (2)	216 (2)
Central	160 (2)	206 (1)	220 (2)
West	157 (1)	203 (2)	217 (1)
Size/Type Community			
Rural	153 (2)	203 (3)	213 (3)
Disadvantaged-Urban	142 (2)	188 (2)	201 (2)
Advantaged-Urban	170 (2)	221 (2)	228 (2)

*Standard errors are presented in parentheses. It can be said with 95 percent certainty that the average writing achievement of the population of interest is in the interval of the estimated average ±2 standard errors.

The Relationship Between Reading Proficiency and Writing Achievement

Are better readers also better writers? Since both reading and writing were assessed in 1984, it is possible to relate students' achievement in these two areas. In reporting the reading results for the 1984 assessment, NAEP identified five levels of reading proficiency: rudimentary, basic, intermediate, adept, and advanced.* **Figure 5.2** presents the ARM writing achievement results for students attaining each level of reading proficiency based on the NAEP assessment.

At all three grade levels, students who did well on National Assessment measures of reading proficiency also did well on measures of writing achievement.** More profi-

*The Reading Report Card: Progress Toward Excellence in Our Schools, Trends in Reading over Four National Assessments, 1971-1984. Educational Testing Service, 1985.

**These results are strongly reinforced by the averages of results for the tasks actually administered at each grade level; the differences between the writing achievement of advanced readers and basic readers are roughly twice the values of the corresponding differences using the ARM results. See Procedural Appendix.

Average Writing Achievement (ARM) for Students in Grades 4, 8 and 11 by Reading Proficiency Level

FIGURE 5.2

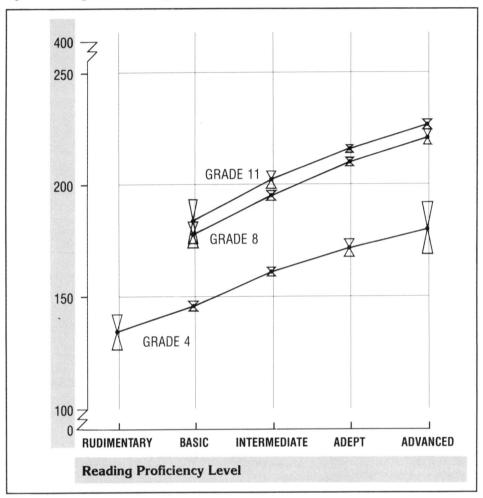

X = estimated average writing achievement and 95 percent confidence interval. It can be said with 95 percent certainty that the average writing achievement of the population of interest is in this interval.

THE NATION'S REPORT CARD

*Results are not presented for the rudimentary reading proficiency level at grades 8 and 11, because all but a few (0.2 percent) eighth graders and all eleventh graders attained at least the basic level of reading proficiency.

cient readers have higher writing achievement, reflecting the integrated nature of literacy skills. This supports the need to provide broad-based home and school experiences, not only in separate reading and writing activities, but also in activities where reading and writing work supportively, leading toward the completion of a particular goal.

Home Influences on Writing Achievement

Much research has been conducted regarding the impact of home environment on student achievement. The NAEP results for three home factors—parents' level of education, reading material in the home, and mother working outside the home—are presented in **Table 5.3.**

TABLE 5.3

Average Writing Achievement (ARM)* for Home Background Factors

	GRADES		
	4	**8**	**11**
Parents' Level of Education			
No high school diploma	143 (3)	189 (2)	199 (2)
Graduated high school	154 (1)	202 (1)	215 (1)
Post-high school	166 (1)	213 (1)	227 (1)
Reading Materials in the Home**			
0-2	147 (1)	186 (2)	197 (3)
3	154 (2)	198 (1)	205 (2)
4	159 (2)	203 (1)	216 (1)
5	164 (1)	210 (1)	223 (1)
Mothers Working Outside the Home			
No	156 (1)	204 (1)	217 (1)
Yes	160 (1)	206 (1)	220 (1)

*Standard errors are presented in parentheses. It can be said with 95 percent certainty that the average writing achievement of the population of interest is in the interval of the estimated average ±2 standard errors.

**Students were asked about five types of reading and reference materials—a dictionary, an encyclopedia, books, newspapers and magazines.

The relationship between parents' level of education and writing achievement is consistent at all three grade levels. Students whose parents have a post-high-school education have substantially higher average writing achievement than do those whose parents have graduated from high school; and the latter are better writers than are those whose parents have not graduated from high school.

That the general level of literacy in the home is related to writing achievement is even more apparent in the results of the series of questions about reading materials in the home. Students were asked about the availability of five types of reading materials in the home: books, newspapers, magazines, a dictionary, and an encyclopedia. At all three grade levels, children from homes with more reading and reference materials had substantially higher average writing achievements than did students who had few such materials available. (The percentages of students reporting no reading materials or only one or two kinds of reading materials at home were 16 percent at grade 4, 6 percent at grade 8, and 4 percent at grade 11.)

In an earlier study, NAEP reported that students whose mothers work outside the home did not have lower reading proficiency.* The writing achievement data also suggest that students whose mothers work outside the home perform at least as well, if not slightly better than, students from homes where mothers stay home. (Fifty-seven percent of the fourth graders, 64 percent of the eighth graders, and 66 percent of the eleventh graders reported that their mothers worked outside the home.) Achievement seems to be more directly related to parents' level of schooling and availability of reading materials than to whether or not the mother works outside the home.

Computers and Writing Achievement

There has been much discussion and speculation about the relationship between using computers to write and level of writing achievement. At all three grade levels, NAEP asked two questions about computers. Student responses are shown in **Table 5.4.** Results indicated that between 24 and 30 percent had computers in their homes. Although the average writing achievement tended to be slightly higher for students with computers at home, these differences may simply be a reflection of socioeconomic level.

TABLE 5.4.

Computers and Average Writing Achievement (ARM)*

	GRADE 4		GRADE 8		GRADE 11	
	% of Students†	Writing Achievement	% of Students†	Writing Achievement	% of Students†	Writing Achievement
Do you have a computer in your home?						
YES	30%	160 (1)	24%	207 (1)	26%	221 (1)
NO	69	158 (1)	75	205 (1)	74	218 (1)
Do you ever use a computer to write stories, papers, or letters?						
YES	21%	151 (5)	15%	204 (4)	21%	223 (4)
NO	79	161 (3)	85	206 (2)	79	218 (2)

*Standard errors are presented in parentheses. It can be said with 95 percent certainty that the average writing achievement of the population of interest is in the interval of the estimated average ±2 standard errors.

†Percents do not total 100 percent due to rounding error.

The second question asked: Do you ever use a computer to write stories, papers, or letters? At all three grades, the percentage of students reporting such use varied between 15 and 21 percent. Relationships to writing achievement were inconsistent and showed only trivial differences in levels of achievement. Students at grades 4 and 8 who reported using a computer to write had slightly lower writing achievement. In contrast, eleventh graders who reported using a computer to write had slightly higher writing achievement. It is likely that computers have been used in the respondents' homes and schools for so short a period of time that it is too soon to determine their effects on children's writing achievement.

Television Viewing and Homework

Low levels of student achievement are frequently attributed to the effects of television, while homework is usually considered beneficial to achievement. NAEP data cannot show cause-and-effect relationships and therefore cannot be used to verify or refute either claim. NAEP, however, did ask questions about television viewing and homework. The results are presented in **Table 5.5.**

At all three grade levels, there was a consistent relationship between television viewing and writing achievement. Zero to two hours a day of television were positively related to writing achievement. The patterns were the same at all three grade levels, with noticeable declines in writing achievement when reported viewing increased to three to five hours a day and further substantial decreases in achievement when reported viewing increased to six hours or more *per day.*

In general, students who received homework assignments and did them tended to have higher writing achievement levels than students who did not have assigned homework or who did not do their assigned homework. The amount of homework associated with the highest achievement levels varied with grade level, however. At grades 4 and 8, the highest achievement levels occurred for students who reported one to two hours of homework per day. At grade 11, the highest achievement levels occurred for students reporting more than two hours of homework. This pattern is similar to that found by NAEP for reading proficiency, and it may be a function of the complexity of the assignments given to the older students.*

A question about number of pages read a day in school and for homework showed similar results. At grades 4 and 8, even though the differences were very slight, the highest writing achievement was for students who reported reading 11 to 15 pages a day. Those who reported reading more had somewhat lower writing achievement. At grade 11, however, students who reported reading more than 20 pages a day for school and homework had the highest writing achievement.

*The Reading Report Card: Progress Toward Excellence in Our Schools, Trends in Reading over Four National Assessments, 1971–1984. Educational Testing Service, 1985.

Average Writing Achievement (ARM)*

	GRADE 4	
	Percent of Students†	Writing Achievement
Hours of Television Viewing Each Day		
0-2 Hours	32%	164 (1)
3-5 Hours	38	160 (1)
6 Hours or More	30	150 (2)
Homework a Day		
None assigned	33%	158 (1)
Did not do it	4	150 (2)
Less than 1 Hour	43	159 (1)
1-2 Hours	14	162 (1)
More than 2 Hours	6	153 (3)
Pages a Day Read for School or Homework		
5	32%	155 (1)
6-10	26	160 (2)
11-15	15	161 (1)
16-20	14	160 (2)
More than 20	13	158 (2)

TABLE 5.5

for Homework and Television Viewing Habits

GRADE 8		GRADE 11	
Percent of Students†	Writing Achievement	Percent of Students†	Writing Achievement
37%	211 (1)	57%	222 (1)
50	207 (1)	37	216 (1)
13	196 (2)	6	207 (2)
22%	203 (1)	21%	213 (1)
4	196 (3)	11	214 (2)
35	207 (1)	26	218 (1)
30	210 (1)	27	222 (1)
9	207 (2)	14	227 (2)
26%	201 (1)	19%	213 (2)
34	207 (1)	26	217 (1)
18	210 (1)	19	220 (2)
10	209 (2)	15	221 (2)
11	205 (2)	21	223 (2)

*Standard errors are presented in parentheses. It can be said with 95 percent certainty that the average writing achievement of the population of interest is in the interval of the estimated average ±2 standard errors.

†Percents do not total 100 percent due to rounding error.

Summary: Performance for Subgroups

Although the demographic factors discussed in this chapter cannot be influenced directly by parents and schools, concerns about levels of achievement can be addressed through programs or special attention to groups of students who need additional instruction. The NAEP data show that the writing achievement of Black and Hispanic students, as well as that of students from disadvantaged-urban communities, is well below that of their White classmates and that of students from advantaged-urban communities.

Other factors investigated in this chapter are ones that schools and parents can attempt to influence directly: Reading materials in the home, reading for school, computer use in writing, the amount of homework and the extent of television watching can be governed to some extent. From this perspective, results from these factors may be even more useful in suggesting further action.

Better readers are better writers. Although most students appear to have access to a variety of reading materials, those who do not have such materials available in the home and those who do not read for school are noticeably poorer writers. Given that better readers are better writers, schools and parents may want to seek ways to provide all students with supplementary reading materials and to encourage reading as well as writing activities. Tasks involving both reading and writing activities may be the most beneficial of all.

In contrast, the results about using a computer to write are far less clear. It may be that while the computer is a useful tool in writing, the use of a computer in and of itself—without good writing instruction—will not improve writing achievement. It is too soon to tell.

Students with higher writing achievement seem to do more homework. This is revealed most clearly at grade 11, where more time spent on homework and more pages read are both related to higher levels of writing achievement.

NAEP results indicate that the majority of eleventh graders and roughly one-third of fourth and eighth graders watch reasonable amounts of television (two hours or less per day) with no apparent negative and perhaps some positive effects on their writing achievement. However, almost one-third of the fourth graders, 13 percent of the eighth graders, and 6 percent of the eleventh graders watch televison excessively (six hours or more per day); the writing achievement of these students is appreciably lower than that of their classmates. While simply reducing the hours students spend in front of the television set is unlikely to improve writing achievement, substituting writing activities, reading, homework, or other literacy experiences for watching television may be helpful. Young children who watch six hours of television a day cannot be doing much else in their spare time, and their literacy skills may suffer as a result.

Part II

The Writing Students Do and the Help They Receive

Because this is an era when schools across the country have increased the priority they place on writing instruction, it seemed particularly timely to describe students' perceptions of their instructional environments and to relate these to writing achievement. Therefore the 1984 writing assessment included more student background questions than ever before. These focused on the students' attitudes toward writing, the strategies they used to complete their writing assignments, the kinds of writing they did in school, and the kinds of instruction and help they reported receiving from their teachers.

The ability to describe such relationships is a direct result of NAEP's new design, which ensures that even though most questions are not given to all students in the NAEP sample, a substantial portion are given to intersecting samples of students. Further, as described in the beginning of Chapter Five, NAEP used a new measurement technique, Average Response Method (ARM) scaling, to estimate the average writing achievement of students at all three grade levels on the same set of 10 informative and persuasive writing tasks—as if students had responded to all 10. With some modification, this same technique was used to estimate students' responses about writing background factors—as if students had answered the full set of questions.

The results of student responses to the questions about their writing practices and instruction are included in the chapters that follow. Additionally, factor-analytic techniques were used to cluster the responses to individual questions into 11 dimensions underlying the students' responses, and factor scores were estimated for students using the ARM scaling procedure.* In order to relate these 11 background measures to writing achievement in a systematic way, the resultant measures were standardized to reflect three levels of student response: low, moderate, and high. These levels are defined with respect to the patterns of students' responses to each cluster of questions. Thus, for each measure, the meaning of "high," "moderate," and "low" has to be considered relative to the patterns of response to the individual items contributing to that measure.

Chapters 6 through 8 focus on the following:

Chapter 6—Values and Attitudes Toward Writing

> Attitude Toward Writing
> Value Placed on Writing
> Writing for Personal Purposes
> Writing for Functional Purposes
> Sharing Work with Others

Chapter 7—Managing the Writing Process

> Use of Planning Strategies
> Use of Revising and Editing Strategies

Chapter 8—Writing Instuction

> Writing in English Class
> Process-Oriented Teaching Activities
> Teacher Comments on Final Paper
> Teacher Feedback

*Since multiple regression procedures were used to create the ARM scale, the results it describes tend to be conservatively estimated. To detect possible stronger relationships where they occur, and to aid in interpreting the findings, all results also have been computed in a second way—as the average of the observed means for each writing task administered at the grade level. This second analysis does not provide for comparisons across grade levels as does the ARM, but it does give unattenuated results within each grade level. Further documentation of the ways in which the results were analyzed, as well as the results for both computational methods and their standard errors, are contained in the Procedural Appendix.

Chapter

Students' Values and Attitudes Toward Writing

Learning to write is a complex process that involves much more than is reflected in the papers students write in response to National Assessment writing tasks. Recognizing this, the writing objectives developed for the 1984 assessment also stated that 1) students should learn to value writing, and 2) students should learn to manage the writing process.* Progress toward these goals will be discussed in this and the following chapter.

As part of the 1984 assessment, students responded to a number of questions designed to assess the value they place on writing. Like the writing tasks discussed in Part I of this report, these questions were administered to systematic samples of students in a way that allowed accurate estimates of responses for the nation as a whole. Questions about valuing writing and writing practice were used to construct several background measures that could be related to writing achievement. The measures discussed in this section include students' attitudes toward writing, the value they see in knowing how to write well, their use of writing for functional and personal purposes, and their sharing of writing with others.

Learning to Value Writing

Tables **6.1** and **6.2** summarize the results for the questions measuring value placed on writing and attitude toward writing.

Value Placed on Writing. This included student reactions to the truth of such statements as "Writing is important," "Writing can help me find a job," and "Writing

---

*Writing Objectives, 1983-84 Assessment, National Assessment of Educational Progress. Education Commission of the States, 1982.

TABLE 6.1

Value Placed on Writing

Statements About Writing	Percentage of Students Reporting the Statements True More Than Half the Time		
	GRADES		
Writing:	4	8	11
1. is important.	78.6	72.6	69.2
2. helps me learn about myself.	53.6	44.6	49.5
3. helps me remind myself and others about things.	61.4	62.0	61.1
4. helps me study.	74.0	71.5	65.9
5. helps me come up with new ideas.	69.6	61.7	59.9
6. helps me think more clearly.	56.1	44.0	51.2
7. helps me tell others what I think.	57.6	50.6	55.3
8. helps tell others what I feel.	54.8	50.3	55.9
9. helps me understand my own feelings.	54.4	43.3	48.4
10. can help me get a good job.	46.0	50.7	57.3
11. helps me share my ideas.	63.5	56.6	61.2
12. helps me show people I know something.	68.4	61.5	62.5
13. People who write well have a better chance of getting good jobs.	53.8	45.7	56.1
14. People who write well are more influential.	51.0	47.4	56.4

helps me remind myself about things." Across the 14 questions included, the results show that perceptions about the value of writing fell slightly between grades 4 and 8, but for some questions recovered to earlier levels by grade 11.

Attitude Toward Writing. This included students' responses to how often each of eight statements such as "I like to write" and "I am a good writer" might apply to themselves. As students move from grade 4 to grade 11, their attitudes toward writing gradually deteriorate: Although 57 percent of the fourth graders reported they like to write the majority of the time, by eleventh grade this decreased to 39 percent.

TABLE 6.2

Attitude Toward Writing

Statements About Writing	Percentage of Students Reporting the Statements True More Than Half the Time*		
	GRADES		
	4	**8**	**11**
1. I like to write.	57.0	41.2	39.4
2. I am a good writer.	57.8	42.1	40.7
3. I think writing is a waste of time.*	19.7	13.5	8.3
4. People like what I write.	53.2	36.5	36.7
5. I write on my own outside of school.	48.2	35.4	28.8
6. I don't like to write things that will be graded.*	36.0	31.7	30.4
7. If I didn't have to write for school, I wouldn't write anything.*	31.4	18.9	16.2
8. Did you like doing the writing for the last thing you wrote for school?*	67.4	57.5	53.6

*Note that questions 3, 6, and 7 are stated negatively and this was accounted for in constructing the factor based on this set of questions. Percents for question 8 are for students responding "yes."

Generally, students do not appear enthusiastic about writing. More students, however, report understanding the value of writing than report liking it or being good at it. They seem to be able to separate their like or dislike of writing from the realization that writing well is a desirable skill.

We can also ask whether there is any relationship between these values and attitudes and students' overall writing achievement. The relevant data are displayed in **Figure 6.1,** which plots the average writing achievement scores for students with differing values and attitudes toward writing.

Figure 6.1 suggests that values and attitudes, as measured in this assessment, are unrelated to writing achievement at grade 4, but show positive relationships by grade 11. Eleventh graders who value writing and have a more positive attitude toward it are also likely to have somewhat higher writing achievement. The NAEP data cannot show whether this is because having a positive attitude toward writing contributes to writing achievement or because writing well leads students to develop more positive attitudes.

Average Writing Achievement (ARM) for Students in Grades 4, 8 and 11 by Value Placed on Writing and Attitude Toward Writing

FIGURE 6.1

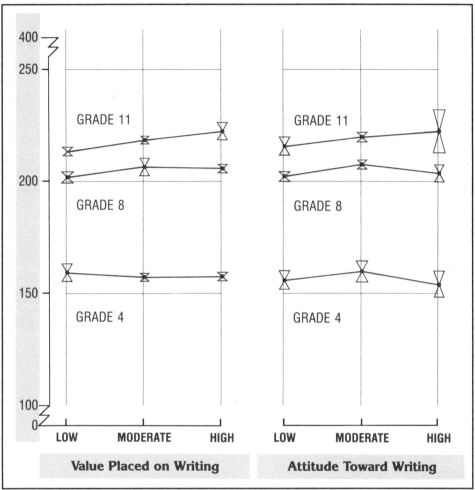

⊠ = estimated average writing achievement and 95 percent confidence interval. It can be said with 95 percent certainty that the average writing achievement of the population of interest is in this interval.

THE NATION'S REPORT CARD

Personal and Functional Uses of Writing

Another set of questions asked about personal and functional uses of writing. Some of these questions asked directly about students' own writing; others asked more generally about the extent to which such writing occurs in the home. The questions yielded two background measures, one reflecting personal writing (such as diaries and letters) and the other reflecting functional writing (such as shopping lists and instructions).

When these summary background measures were being constructed, the patterns of results for individual items concerning the influence of the home were particularly interesting, in that they indicated a close relationship between home and student writing practices. Students tend to use writing in the same way their families do. For example, if the people they live with keep diaries, the students are likely to do so too.

Results for most of the questions about personal and functional writing are presented in **Tables 6.3** and **6.4.** Table 6.3 contains results for questions that reflect how often the students and the people they live with write for personal or social purposes. Reports of student and family personal and social writing were fairly consistent across the three grade levels, with the exception of an increase in note and message writing in the eleventh grade. Perhaps as students grow older and more independent, leaving notes becomes a more frequent method of communication among family members. The other interesting result is the decrease in writing stories and poems for pleasure reported between grade 4 and grade 8. This is consistent with the increasingly negative attitude toward writing displayed by older students.

TABLE 6.3

Personal/Social Writing by Students and the People They Live With

| | Percentage of Students Reporting At Least Weekly Activity | | |
| | GRADES | | |
Personal/Social Uses	4	8	11
How often do the people you live with:			
Keep diaries or journals?	23.0	19.4	17.4
Write letters to friends?	34.3	34.3	37.3
Write notes and messages?	44.1	61.1	74.8
How often do you:			
Keep a diary or journal?	36.4	27.3	20.7
Write letters to friends?	36.0	38.7	39.5
Write notes and messages?	44.1	68.9	75.3
Write stories or poems that aren't schoolwork?	27.8	11.2	12.8

Table 6.4 contains results for questions included in the measure of how often students and the people they live with write for more functional reasons. Although the amount of functional writing they report their families do is fairly consistent across grade levels, students report a decrease in their own functional writing, particularly between grades 4 and 8.

Relationships between these background measures and writing achievement are displayed in **Figure 6.2.** Particularly at ages 8 and 11, students who indicated that they and the people they live with wrote more frequently for personal and social purposes also tended to have higher writing achievement. For functional writing, however, the relationships between achievement and frequency are inconsistent. This may be because people are more likely to write for functional reasons out of practical necessity, whereas writing for personal and social purposes is a matter of choice. It may be that poor writers as well as good ones frequently need to write forms, lists, and messages in their daily lives, but that good writers are more likely to elect to write letters and keep journals.

TABLE 6.4

Functional Uses of Writing by Students and the People They Live With

	Percentage of Students Reporting At Least Weekly Activity		
	GRADES		
Functional Uses	4	8	11
How often do the people you live with:			
Make lists of things to buy or do?	62.4	67.8	71.7
Copy recipes or directions?	37.5	31.0	30.8
Fill out order blanks?	29.4	23.8	25.1
How often do you:			
Make lists of things to buy or do?	54.8	44.5	46.3
Copy recipes or directions?	37.6	23.7	18.3
Fill out order blanks?	29.2	17.9	15.6
Write for the school newspaper, magazine, or yearbook?	12.5	7.2	5.5

Average Writing Achievement (ARM) for Students in Grades 4, 8 and 11 by Personal/Social Writing and Functional Writing

FIGURE 6.2

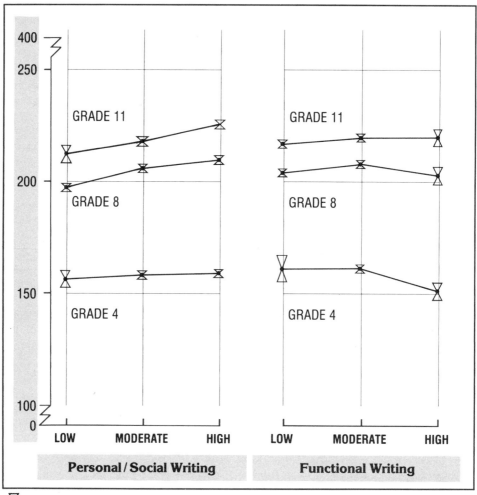

$\times$ = estimated average writing achievement and 95 percent confidence interval. It can be said with 95 percent certainty that the average writing achievement of the population of interest is in this interval.

Sharing Writing with Others

The rewards of sharing one's work with others can make the effort of writing worthwhile. Conversely, refusing to share one's writing is likely to reflect disinterest or lack of confidence in the work or a mistrust of the value that others place on what one has written.

Three questions measured how and to what extent students shared their writing with friends, with their families, or with broader audiences through a school newspaper. The percentages are summarized in **Table 6.5.**

TABLE 6.5

Sharing Writing with Others

Sharing Writing	Percentage of Students Who Report Sharing Their Writing At Least Half the Time		
	GRADES		
	4	**8**	**11**
With friends	56.5	63.3	58.6
With the people in your family	82.8	67.9	50.3
Printed in a school newspaper	20.6	6.8	5.6

At grade 4, 83 percent of the students reported that they shared their work with their families at least half the time, and 57 percent shared work with their friends. Fewer students (21 percent) were likely to have published pieces in a school newspaper. By grade 11, students were markedly less likely to report sharing work with their parents, with only 50 percent tending to do so, and were even less likely to have had it published in a school paper, with only about 6 percent having had work printed. Since friends and family are usually easily accessible audiences for writing that students want to share, it may be reasonable to interpret these results as a reflection of the decreasing interest that parents and fellow students place on their own children's and peers' work. However, since the students themselves have less positive attitudes toward writing, they are probably less likely to share what they have written, and therefore parents and friends may not be given many opportunities to read students' writing.

On the other hand, finding broader audiences for one's writing appears to be positively related to writing achievement at grades 8 and 11 (**Figure 6.3**). Students who share their work tend to have higher average writing achievement. Parent as well as student behavior may contribute to these patterns. While parents ask to see their children's papers in the lower grades, they may stop doing this as their children grow older. Such behavior may be interpreted by the older students as parental disinterest in their school writing. Better writers may still seek those opportunities, however, and the families of better writers may encourage it, thus creating a context in which audiences are more available and in which there is a better chance of the students becoming even better writers.

Average Writing Achievement (ARM) for Students in Grades 4, 8 and 11 by Sharing Writing with Others

FIGURE 6.3

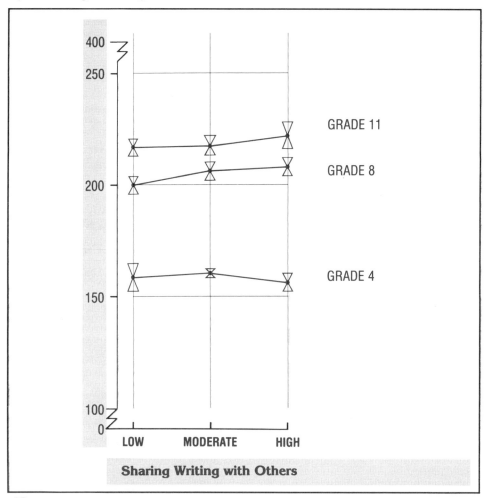

$\underline{\mathbb{X}}$ = estimated average writing achievement and 95 percent confidence interval. It can be said with 95 percent certainty that the average writing achievement of the population of interest is in this interval.

THE NATION'S REPORT CARD

Summary: Valuing Writing

The results discussed in this chapter suggest that the majority of students seem to recognize that writing can serve a variety of useful purposes, both personal and social. They do not necessarily *like* to write, however, and their attitudes toward writing show a steady deterioration across the grades, as does their propensity to seek broader audiences for their writing. This is particularly disturbing, because the results also show that by grade 11 the students with more positive attitudes also tend to be better writers.

Chapter **7**

Managing the Writing Process

Any piece of writing has its own process of development over time, a history of the author gathering and organizing information, exploring relationships among new ideas, drafting, revising, and editing for particular audiences or purposes. In any specific writing activity, these processes will be intertwined, with one or another receiving primary emphasis, depending upon the writer's sense of how the whole piece is progressing.

Experienced writers develop a wide variety of strategies and approaches for generating ideas, drafting new material, revising what they have written, and editing for accuracy. Writers can insert additional information to support a point, rearrange their work by cutting and pasting, abandon a draft and start again, ask others to respond to work in progress, outline a rough draft to assess how well it is organized, or use a word processor to edit. Even simple strategies such as cutting and pasting are not obvious to novices. Indeed, learning to manage the process is an important part of learning to write.

Recent discussions of writing instruction have recognized the importance of the writing process and have advocated instructional activities that focus on one or another aspect of what writers do.* Because of these concerns, the 1984 assessment included a number of questions about how students went about completing their writing assignments. Responses to these questions yielded two measures that NAEP has related to writing achievement—one reflecting planning activities and the other focusing on the strategies students use for revising and editing. The results for additional student questions about the extent to which their teachers used process-oriented instructional activities and how these activities relate to achievement will be examined in Chapter 8.

What Works: Research About Teaching and Learning, U.S. Department of Education, 1986.

Planning

Four questions about different aspects of planning were used to develop this measure, and the results of all four are summarized in **Table 7.1.** Across all three grade levels, 81 to 85 percent of the students reported that most of the time they thought before writing. Fewer, from 44 to 63 percent, reported relatively frequent use of the other three more specific strategies included in the table—asking oneself about the subject, looking up additional information, and thinking about different audiences.

Across grades, the more general the strategy, the more likely it was to be reported by the students. This may suggest that students are less likely to engage in detailed planning or that they are unfamiliar with the techniques that can be used to consider various aspects of a paper's subject and audience.

Differences among grade levels in the reported use of planning were slight for most strategies. Looking up facts, however, increased somewhat (from 48 to 62 percent) between grades 4 and 11. This probably reflects a shift toward more academic writing in the upper grades.

Use of Planning Strategies Reported by Students

TABLE 7.1

	Percentage of Students Reporting Use More Than Half of the Time		
	GRADES		
Planning Strategies	4	8	11
How often do you:			
Think before writing?	81.2	84.1	85.2
Ask yourself about the subject?	55.9	47.0	52.1
Look up facts?	47.9	55.8	63.3
Write differently for different audiences?	47.8	44.4	43.6

Figure 7.1 displays the relationships between the amount of planning students reported and their average writing achievement. There is little apparent relationship between planning and writing achievement at grade 4, but eighth-grade students who reported more planning tended to have slightly higher achievement scores.* By

*This interpretation is reinforced by the results for the averages of the observed results for the tasks actually administered at grade 8. See Procedural Appendix.

FIGURE 7.1

Average Writing Achievement (ARM) for Students in Grades 4, 8 and 11 by Use of Planning Strategies

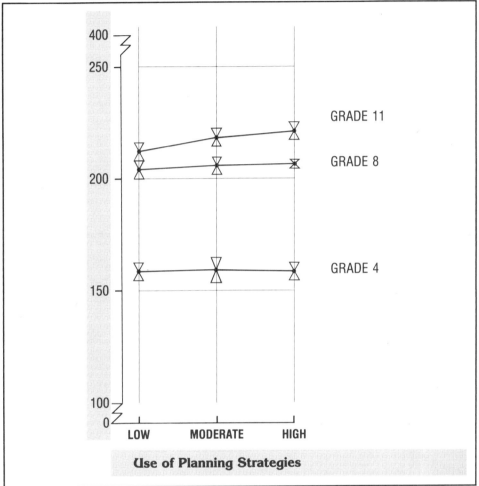

X = estimated average writing achievement and 95 percent confidence interval. It can be said with 95 percent certainty that the average writing achievement of the population of interest is in this interval.

THE NATION'S REPORT CARD

eleventh grade the students who reported more planning also had systematically higher writing-achievement scores.

Self-reports such as these are useful in examining relative emphasis on different approaches and differences in emphasis across groups. They do not necessarily provide a good indication of how much use students really make of such strategies. Three of the persuasive writing tasks included in the assessment explicitly gave the students an opportunity to plan before they wrote (Aunt May, Recreational Opportunity, and Uncle). The formats for these assignments were similar: The task (or prompt) was printed at the top of the page, and the remainder of the page was left blank for the students to make notes before writing. (The writing itself was to be done on the next page.) In addition to rating the writing that resulted, readers also tabulated whether the students had used the space provided to make notes.

The results of these tabulations are presented in **Table 7.2.** Even when students were explicitly given the opportunity to make notes to use in planning their assessment responses, few did so. At grade 4, only 8 percent of the students made notes; even at grade 11, only 19 to 20 percent of the students wrote something down to help them in formulating their persuasive letters. The differences from grade 4 to the higher grades in using this planning strategy are substantial, but the amount of recorded planning is considerably less than the self-reports might suggest.

Recorded Planning in Writing Assessment Responses

TABLE 7.2

	Percentage of Students Who Made Notes When Given the Space and Opportunity		
	GRADES		
Writing Task	4	8	11
Aunt May	8.1	—	—
Recreational Opportunity	—	16.5	18.8
Uncle	—	—	19.8

Revising and Editing Strategies

Fourteen questions asked about students' strategies for revising and editing what they had written. Use of these 14 strategies at each grade level is summarized in **Table 7.3.**

Overall, students reported more use of revising and editing strategies in the upper grades than they did in the lower. However, even at grade 4 the strategies reported are relatively extensive. Sixty percent of the fourth graders reported that they made some changes in their last paper before handing it in, and 69 percent reported that they made at least some changes while writing the majority of their papers. On another question, 74 percent indicated that they corrected errors in spelling.

At the same time, at all three grade levels the kinds of revising and editing reported are closely tied to the effort involved. The most frequently reported strategies involve the smallest units of the text—spelling, punctuation, and other changes that can be

Use of Revising and Editing Strategies Reported by Students

TABLE 7.3

Revising and Editing Strategies Overall	Percentage of Students Reporting Use More Than Half of the Time*		
	GRADES		
	4	**8**	**11**
Did you:			
Recopy last paper before handing it in?	45.6	66.8	74.7
Make changes in last paper before handing it in?	60.2	77.5	83.6
How often do you:			
Make changes as you write?	69.3	74.0	77.4
Make changes after you have written the paper once?	55.7	68.2	70.9
Think about where different facts and ideas go in the paper?	66.0	67.6	75.8
Units of Revision			
Correct spelling	73.9	75.1	75.1
Correct punctuation	63.1	68.2	67.4
Correct grammar	50.6	66.5	69.2
Change words	64.9	68.5	72.1
Add ideas or information	62.1	62.1	67.4
Take out parts you don't like	46.5	56.0	61.6
Move sentences or paragraphs	39.0	36.4	46.0
Rewrite most of the paper	31.8	42.1	43.8
Throw out your paper and start again	31.0	33.3	27.8

*Percentages for first two questions are for students responding "yes."

made while writing. The lowest percentages in Table 7.3 are for strategies that require extensive effort—starting over, rewriting most of the paper, moving sentences around, taking out parts, and adding ideas or information. Thus, students report far more use of editing strategies than of revision strategies.

Thinking about where ideas and facts go in the paper was more closely aligned with revision than with planning, and more students reported making revisions while writing than after having completed a draft of a paper. This may reflect a kind of in-process adjustment to writing plans, which lessens the need for more extensive revision later. On the other hand, it may be that students need more guidance in the use of planning and revising strategies that require taking a broader view of a paper and evaluating its overall organization and coherence.

Average Writing Achievement (ARM) for Students in Grades 4, 8 and 11 by Use of Revising and Editing Strategies

FIGURE 7.2

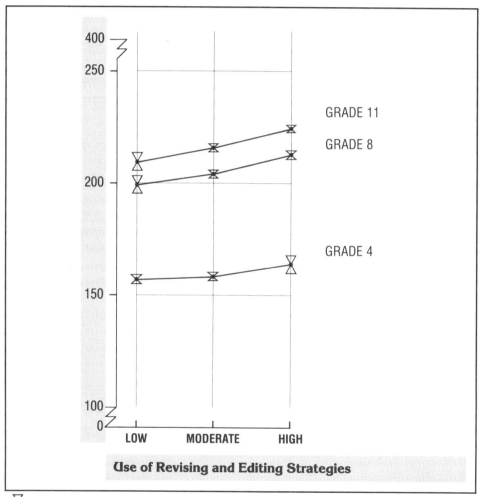

$\overline{\underline{X}}$ = estimated average writing achievement and 95 percent confidence interval. It can be said with 95 percent certainty that the average writing achievement of the population of interest is in this interval.

Relationships between revising and editing strategies and average writing achievement are displayed in **Figure 7.2.**

At all three grades, students who reported making more use of these strategies were likely to have received higher writing achievement scores. Especially at grades 8 and 11, students who are better writers seem to have incorporated revising and editing strategies into their writing process.

Summary: Managing the Writing Process

Students' reports of the strategies they adopt to govern their writing suggest that they employ a variety of planning, revising, and editing strategies. The use of such strategies increases between grades 4 and 11, though even at grade 4 a considerable percentage of the students reported using relevant writing strategies. Further, these strategies are generally associated with higher writing achievement at each grade. Thus, NAEP data support the idea that teaching students the strategies involved in the writing process will improve writing achievement.

Still, the writing process—planning, revising, and editing—is not routine for all students. About half the students at all three grade levels reported that most of the time they do not make detailed plans, and less than 20 percent made notes about what they might write. About 25 percent of the eleventh graders and even more of the fourth and eighth graders reported that most of the time they do not revise and edit.

More importantly, although students report that they plan, revise, and edit their writing, it is not certain that they are doing these things effectively. Students seem well aware that they should be planning, revising, and editing what they write, but the papers they write are often strikingly ineffective. Further, students tend to use these strategies at a superficial level (e.g., general planning rather than specific and revision involving changes in words and punctuation rather than in overall organization). Only 46 percent of the eleventh graders reported they were likely to move sentences and paragraphs in completing their writing assignments.

The reports on the writing process may help clarify the task facing the nation's teachers: It will not be enough to teach students that they should plan, revise, and edit their work. Those are strategies that students believe they are using already. Instead, teachers need to help students understand these processes more fully and manage them more effectively. This is a different and perhaps harder task: to extend and elaborate on approaches that may be relatively firmly ingrained, to help students understand that there may be more than one approach to a task, and to teach them how to choose among the alternatives.

Chapter

Writing Instruction: What Students Write in School and the Help They Receive

---

To understand better the state of writing achievement in school-age children, it is useful to look beyond the students' writing samples, attitudes, and writing strategies to the factors that influence them in school. Part I of this report emphasized that students must learn to use writing to accomplish many different purposes, from letters requesting the correction of a billing error, to reports on recent experiences, to arguments in defense of a particular course of action or point of view. This chapter will focus on the extent to which students' school experiences are introducing them to a range of purposes for writing and the types of instruction that are being provided to strengthen their skills as writers.

To examine these issues, the 1984 assessment included a variety of questions asking students about how much they write for school, about their perceptions of the types of writing they do in their classes, and about the kinds of instruction and feedback they receive.

How Frequently Students Write in School

To obtain a general measure of how much writing students do for school, NAEP asked students how many reports and essays they had written in the last six weeks for *any school subject.* The results are shown in **Table 8.1.**

TABLE 8.1

Number of Reports and Essays Written During Previous Six Weeks for All School Subjects

	Percentage of Students Reporting Numbers of Reports and Essays Written		
	GRADES		
Number of Essays and Reports	**4**	**8**	**11**
0	20.9%	11.6%	9.3%
1-2	26.1	26.3	27.5
3-4	14.6	21.0	27.3
5-10	19.8	25.5	28.1
More than 10	18.6	15.6	7.8

As can be seen from Table 8.1, most students report doing at least some writing for school. A large proportion of students, however, are not writing very much. About half the fourth graders (47 percent) and more than one-third of the eighth and eleventh graders (38 and 37 percent) reported writing two or fewer reports or essays over the previous six weeks. This averages out to less than one such writing assignment every three weeks.

The relationship between writing achievement as estimated by the ARM scaling method and amount of writing in school is shown in **Figure 8.1.** * In grades 8 and 11 particularly, students who reported doing some writing in school had higher writing achievement than those who reported doing no writing. The most dramatic difference in writing achievement appeared between students who reported no writing and those who reported having written three or four essays and reports in the previous six weeks. For all three grade levels, as the number of essays and reports written increased, so did writing achievement, up to about four, where achievement leveled off or declined with increased numbers of written assignments.

It may be that some students are given a greater number of shorter writing assignments, while others are given fewer, more substantial assignments and are asked to work on them longer. Even though doing at least some writing in school is associated with higher writing achievement, the number and complexity of the assignments

*The results based on the averages across the tasks actually administered at each age differ slightly, though they also show a generally positive relationship between achievement and amount of writing. See Procedural Appendix.

students are given must be carefully considered. It may be reasonable to assign students more short pieces, but NAEP results suggest that students need experience in writing extended, elaborated pieces—with time to think them through and help in producing them.

What Students Write in School

The kinds of writing most students do in school can be divided into two broad categories—content-based writing that focuses on providing information or develop-

FIGURE 8.1

Average Writing Achievement (ARM) for Students in Grades 4, 8 and 11 by Number of Reports and Essays

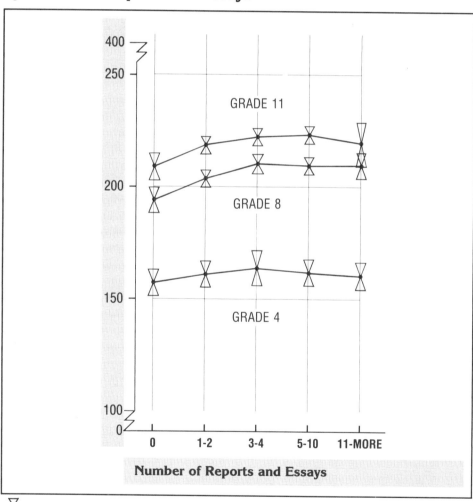

⊠ = estimated average writing achievement and 95 percent confidence interval. It can be said with 95 percent certainty that the average writing achievement of the population of interest is in this interval.

THE NATION'S REPORT CARD

ing an argument (including the informative and persuasive writing tasks discussed in Part I) and imaginative writing that emphasizes creative use of language (whether fictional or based on personal experiences). Informative and persuasive writing often takes the form of reports and essays, whereas imaginative writing is often assigned in the form of stories or poems.

What types of writing did the students report doing for school? **Table 8.2** summarizes responses to a question about the most recent paper the students had written. Across grades, each of the various types of writing received at least some attention. However, content-based informative and persuasive writing predominated and received increasingly heavy emphasis in the upper grades. At fourth grade, 64 percent of the students reported that their most recent piece of writing was likely to have been informative, while 36 percent reported it was a story, poem, or play (imaginative writing). By eleventh grade, 88 percent of the students reported informative and persuasive writing largely in the form of essays (50 percent), but only 12 percent reported that their latest paper was imaginative.

TABLE 8.2

What was the last paper you wrote for school?

	Percentage of Students Reporting Each Kind of Writing		
	GRADES		
Informative and Persuasive Writing	**4**	**8**	**11**
Essays	11.7%	29.1%	49.5%
Book Reports	15.5	23.3	14.5
Other Reports	22.0	17.0	18.0
Letters	14.8	10.4	5.6
Imaginative			
Stories	27.7	16.0	7.6
Poems	6.3	3.3	3.6
Plays	2.0	0.8	1.2

Reports from the fourth graders suggest that their writing may reflect a broader range than in the upper grades. At grade 4, five types of writing assignments were reported by 10 percent or more of the students: stories (28 percent), general reports (22 percent), book reports (16 percent), letters (15 percent), and essays (12 percent). By eleventh grade, only three types of writing were reported by 10 percent or more of the students—essays (50 percent), general reports (18 percent), and book reports (15 percent). This reflects a decreased emphasis on imaginative writing and an increased focus on academic forms in the secondary school, to the exclusion of almost all other forms of writing by eleventh grade.

Writing for English and Language Arts

Results discussed thus far were based on papers students had written for all their classes. Students were also asked about how much of each type of writing they had done in their English classes during the previous week.

Table 8.3 displays the results. For informative and persuasive writing, changes across the grades parallel those already observed. In particular, there is a steady increase in the amount of essay writing, from 21 percent of the students reporting this type of writing in grade 4 to 59 percent in grade 11. However, reports of imaginative writing (particularly stories and plays) remain relatively constant across the grades.

Did you do each of the following kinds of writing for your English class last week?

TABLE 8.3

| | Percentage of Students Reporting at Least One Paper | | |
| | GRADES | | |
Informative and Persuasive Writing	4	8	11
Essays	21.0%	41.0%	58.9%
Book Reports	36.8	34.9	30.5
Other Reports	28.2	26.0	36.4
Letters	39.1	19.9	16.2
Imaginative Writing			
Stories	39.0	40.6	39.1
Poems	26.6	13.9	19.2
Plays	13.4	10.0	12.5

Writing Across the Curriculum

To provide students with more frequent and varied opportunities to write, teachers of subjects other than English have been encouraged to incorporate writing into their class activities. More frequent essay writing in grade 11, reported earlier, may be one result of teachers' response to this call. To explore this issue further, students were asked questions about school writing for two subjects other than English—science and social studies.

Table 8.4 summarizes the results for these two questions and suggests that the call for writing in subjects other than English is being heeded to some degree. The majority of students who took science or social studies reported doing some writing for those classes during the preceding week. The numbers of assignments students report writing each week, however, suggest that many of these assignments are quite short.

Writing Assignments Last Week for Social Studies and Science

TABLE 8.4

	Percentage of Students Reporting Having Assignments		
	GRADES		
How many assignments last week for social studies class?	4	8	11
Don't have a social studies class	8.3%	9.5%	17.8%
NO assignments	21.4	13.4	20.2
ONE assignment	20.3	13.8	19.7
TWO assignments	18.0	18.4	19.6
THREE or MORE	32.0	44.9	22.7
How many assignments last week for science class?			
Don't have a science class	10.8%	12.8%	45.3%
NO assignments	32.8	14.7	13.1
ONE assignment	18.9	12.5	11.5
TWO assignments	16.6	20.4	13.5
THREE or MORE	20.9	39.6	16.6

To sum up, students who reported having written at least three essays or reports during a six-week period had higher writing achievement than those who reported little or no writing. Further, some of this writing seems to be for academic areas other than English. The types of writing students do for school narrow somewhat between grades 4 and 11; the high school years are marked by more essay writing. Imaginative writing (including stories, poems, and plays) receives less attention in the high school years, although students still perceive such writing to be a regular part of their instruction in English.

Process-Oriented Teaching Activities

During the past decade, teachers of English have shifted the emphasis in writing instruction away from reacting to and reworking the finished product toward focusing on the processes students engage in as they write. The previous chapter reported results from students' descriptions of their own writing processes and, in general, found that a broader repertoire of writing strategies was associated with higher average writing achievement. Students were also asked a variety of questions designed to reflect the extent to which they were encountering process-oriented writing instruction: Did their teachers ask them to engage in prewriting activities such as note taking or outlining? Did their teachers provide feedback to work in progress, either through conferences or peer response to student work? Did their teachers emphasize and ask for revisions or multiple drafts? (In contrast to the questions discussed in the preceding chapter, these questions focused specifically on the teachers' instructions rather than on the strategies students typically used while writing.)

Table 8.5 displays the students' responses to questions about process-oriented teaching activities. Between 20 and 27 percent of the fourth graders reported being encouraged to use these activities more than half the time, and this increased substantially across the grade levels for most activities. By grade 11, over 40 percent of the students reported that they were asked to talk with their teachers about their writing and were asked to use such prewriting and revision activities as making notes or outlines

Teachers' Encouragement of the Writing Process

TABLE 8.5

| Process-Oriented Activities | Percentage of Students Reporting Being Asked to Use Activity More Than Half of the Time | | |
| | GRADES | | |
	4	8	11
Make notes before you write	23.7%	41.5%	56.0%
Make an outline	19.7	27.4	47.5
Make notes about changes in the paper	21.4	29.8	39.4
Talk to teacher while writing paper	27.0	29.1	42.0
Talk to classmates while writing paper	21.0	25.9	33.5
Rewrite before the paper is graded	25.9	44.9	57.1
Rewrite after the paper is graded	22.1	14.8	20.8

and rewriting a paper before handing it in. These responses indicate that a growing proportion of students is being asked to perform one or another type of process-oriented writing activity. The percentages, however, do not indicate that instruction encouraging the writing process is routine. For most assignments, the majority of students are not asked to engage in process-oriented writing activities.

Further, evidence that some of these activities have been incorporated into the school day does not necessarily mean that they will be related to writing achievement. **Figure 8.2** displays the relationship between average writing achievement and the amount of process-oriented instruction reported by the students.

**Average Writing Achievement (ARM)
for Students in Grades 4, 8 and 11
by Extent of Process-Oriented Teaching Activities**

FIGURE 8.2

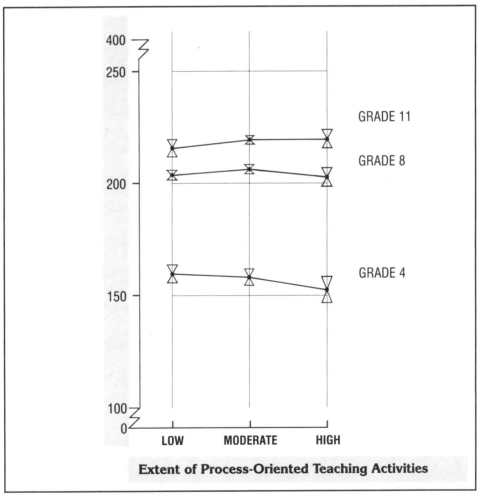

Extent of Process-Oriented Teaching Activities

⋈ = estimated average writing achievement and 95 percent confidence interval. It can be said with 95 percent certainty that the average writing achievement of the population of interest is in this interval.

THE NATION'S
REPORT
CARD

81

At grade 4, students reporting greater engagement in process activities performed less well than classmates who reported less exposure to such activities. At grade 8, students reporting moderate engagement in process activities did better than those receiving lower or higher exposure to such instruction. Only at grade 11 does there seem to be some positive relationship between higher achievement in writing and the teachers' focus on process-related instructional activities **(Figure 8.2)**.

These findings may suggest that process approaches have been superficial rather than unsuccessful. At their best, process approaches are meant to provide students with new and more powerful ways of *thinking* about the information they wish to convey, as well as the writing techniques to do this most successfully. Simply providing students with exposure to new activities (whether revision exercises, peer response groups, or prewriting sessions) may not be enough to ensure that students learn how to use these skills effectively. Students may need more direct instruction in when and how to use such approaches in their own writing and more practice in actual writing situations.

Focusing Instruction on the Finished Product

Students were also asked about the extent to which their teachers commented (either in writing or by talking to them) on their finished papers. These questions included concerns with neatness, word choice, organization, and effectiveness of the completed writing.

The responses to these questions are presented in **Table 8.6.** The results indicate that there is a gradually diminishing focus on some aspects of the final product across the grades. For example, 65 percent of the fourth-grade students reported that their teachers tended to comment on how they had followed directions, whereas only 29 percent of the eleventh graders reported this emphasis. A similar pattern emerged for teachers' concerns with the length and neatness of the finished paper. Such emphases may be appropriate in the early years, when teachers are helping their students learn to make such judgments for themselves, and less necessary in the upper grades.

Emphases on other aspects of the final product remain relatively constant or show only slight decreases between grades 4 and 11. More constant concerns include the ideas and feelings expressed, the adequacy of the explanations presented, word choice, spelling, punctuation, and grammar. These may be the kinds of issues that remain relevant for all students—as their material becomes more complex, they face greater problems in organizing and presenting what they wish to convey. However, the reports indicate that teachers comment more frequently on mechanics—spelling, punctuation, and grammar—than they do on ideas and how to express them. This may partly explain why students tend to change or fix these smaller units of their papers more frequently than they engage in more substantial revision activities (see Chapter 7).

Figure 8.3 displays the relationships between such product-based concerns and average writing achievement. At all three grade levels, increased emphasis on the finished product was inversely associated with writing achievement, probably because

Teachers' Focus on the Finished Product

TABLE 8.6

	Percentage of Students Reporting Teachers Comment on Aspect More Than Half of the Time		
	GRADES		
Aspect of Paper	**4**	**8**	**11**
Follow Directions	65.0%	43.7%	29.3%
Wrote Enough	51.2	36.1	26.2
Ideas in Paper	50.4	43.1	43.0
Way Ideas Explained	49.2	41.1	42.6
Way Feelings Expressed	44.6	34.6	34.0
Organization	50.2	44.2	44.5
Words	51.2	40.0	37.3
Spelling, Punctuation, and Grammar	57.9	56.7	50.6
Neatness and Handwriting	62.8	49.5	30.0

teachers focus such instruction on poorer writers. It is reasonable to assume that poorer writers present finished papers with more opportunities for comment; and it might be expected that teachers would center their efforts on these papers.*

*In considering the results of both computational methods (see Procedural Appendix), this seems to be particularly prevalent at grade 4, where poorer writers systematically reported an increase in the amount of teacher comments on their papers. The differences were less pronounced at grades 8 and 11, although poorer writers tended to report more teacher comments than the better writers.

FIGURE 8.3

Average Writing Achievement (ARM) for Students in Grades 4, 8 and 11 by Extent Teacher Comments on Final Paper

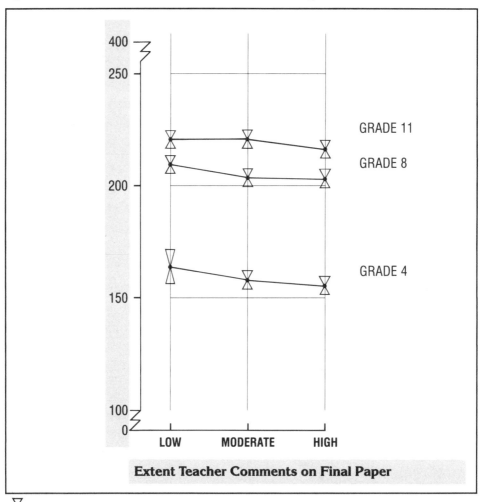

Extent Teacher Comments on Final Paper

 = estimated average writing achievement and 95 percent confidence interval. It can be said with 95 percent certainty that the average writing achievement of the population of interest is in this interval.

THE NATION'S
REPORT
CARD

84

Teacher Feedback

The last set of student reports relates to the kinds and amount of feedback students receive from their teachers. Does the teacher usually mark mistakes, point out good things in the paper, and express interest in what the student had to say?

Results for the six questions are summarized in **Table 8.7.** Marking errors seems to be the most frequent find of feedback at all grades; the percentage of students reporting this occurs most of the time increases across the grades—44 percent at grade 4, 57 percent at grade 8, and 68 percent at grade 11. The increase in negative feedback reported by the older students may partially explain the deterioration of attitudes toward writing by the eleventh grade.

TABLE 8.7

Teachers' Feedback on Student Writing

	Percentage of Students Reporting Teachers Provide Type of Feedback *Almost Every Time* They Write		
	GRADES		
Type of Feedback	**4**	**8**	**11**
Mark mistakes in paper	43.8%	56.8%	68.3%
Write notes on paper	13.8	23.7	47.3
Point out what is well done	30.1	23.4	33.1
Point out what is not well done	27.5	38.4	48.0
Make suggestions for next time	30.5	29.6	34.0
Show an interest in what you write	36.7	29.7	32.1

The teachers' use of written notes on student papers also increases dramatically across the grades (14 percent at grade 4, 24 percent at grade 8, and 47 percent at grade 11). Students reported slightly less overt display of teacher interest at grade 11 than at grade 4, but they also reported receiving slightly more suggestions about ways to change their papers. Students' perceptions of their teachers' interest in what they write are disturbing, in that only 30 to 37 percent of the students reported such teacher interest on a routine basis. While teachers may be more interested than students recognize, the NAEP results indicate that students need more supportive instruction than they perceive themselves to be receiving.

Average Writing Achievement (ARM) for Students in Grades 4, 8 and 11 by Amount of Teacher Feedback

FIGURE 8.4

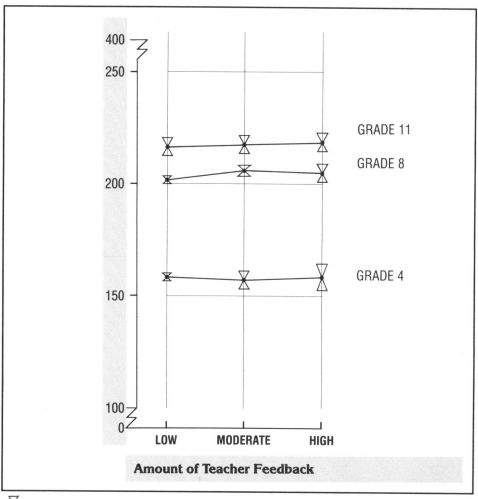

$\underline{\underline{\times}}$ = estimated average writing achievement and 95 percent confidence interval. It can be said with 95 percent certainty that the average writing achievement of the population of interest is in this interval.

THE NATION'S
REPORT
CARD

We can also examine the relationship between the amount of feedback and average writing achievement. (See **Figure 8.4.**) At grade 4, there appears to be little relationship between teacher feedback and writing achievement. At grade 8, the relationship seems to shift. Students who reported little feedback on their work also tended to have lower average writing achievement. However, the students who reported a "medium" amount of feedback had slightly higher writing achievement than those who reported more feedback. By grade 11, it appears that, as the amount of teacher feedback increases, so does the level of writing achievement.*

Summary

Assessment findings regarding writing instruction are mixed. Academic writing is important for the nation's students to learn, and this seems to predominate in school, especially in the later years. However, it seems to be accomplished at the expense of student practice with more literary or imaginative forms. If we want high school graduates to be well-rounded in their writing abilities, we may need to reconsider the balance of content-based and imaginative writing types *and* the range of content areas.

Assessment findings indicate that writing across the curriculum and process-oriented activities have begun to be incorporated into instructional programs across the nation, even if many students receive such instruction rather infrequently. Some students did report extensive exposure to process-oriented writing activities, yet the writing achievement of these students was not consistently higher than that of students who did not report receiving such instruction. While the data are insufficient to lead us to reject these attempts at reform, they do raise questions about the manner in which process activities are being carried out. Are teachers focusing their efforts on the poorer writers? Are teachers assigning more activities and shorter writing tasks to the poorer writers, while the better writers work on more substantive essays and reports? Or are process activities being incorporated into classrooms at the expense of more rigorous writing assignments? Rather than simply adding more process activities, we may need to develop more systematic approaches to process instruction. Such activities should help students monitor and manage *what* and *how* they write. They should provide students with more effective ways to carry out more challenging assignments. How to bring this about needs to be the next order of business for educational researchers, curriculum developers, and teacher trainers alike.

*Even though this relationship is weak in the results from the ARM analysis, the second computational method shows a strong relationship. Based on that method, the average writing achievement of eleventh graders increases substantially— from 195 for those students reporting little feedback to 208 for students reporting moderate feedback and to 218 for students reporting the most feedback from teachers about how to improve their writing.

Procedural Appendix

A Description of the 1983-84 NAEP Writing Assessment

General Background About NAEP, *The Nation's Report Card*

The National Assessment of Educational Progress (NAEP) is an ongoing, congressionally mandated project established to conduct national surveys of the educational attainments of young Americans. Its primary goal is to determine and report the status of and trends over time in educational achievement. NAEP was initiated in 1969 to obtain comprehensive and dependable national educational achievement data in a uniform, scientific manner. Today, NAEP remains the only regularly conducted national survey of educational achievement at the elementary, middle, and high school levels.

Since 1969, NAEP has assessed 9-year-olds, 13-year-olds, and 17-year-olds. In 1983, NAEP began assessing students by grade as well as by age. In addition, NAEP periodically surveys young adults. The subject areas assessed have included reading, writing, mathematics, science, and social studies, as well as citizenship, literature, art, music, and career development. Assessments were conducted annually through 1980 and have been conducted biennially since then. All subjects except career development have been reassessed to determine trends in achievement over time. To date, NAEP has assessed approximately 1,300,000 young Americans.

NAEP completed a young adult literacy assessment in 1985. The 1986 effort included in-school assessments of mathematics, reading, science, and computer competence, along with special probes of U.S. history and literature.

From its inception, NAEP has developed assessments through a consensus process. Educators, scholars, and citizens representative of many diverse constituencies and points of view design objectives for each subject area assessment, proposing general goals they feel students should achieve in the course of their education. After careful reviews, the objectives are given to item writers, who develop assessment questions appropriate to the objectives.

All exercises undergo extensive reviews by subject-matter and measurement specialists, as well as careful scrutiny to eliminate any potential bias or lack of sensitivity to particular groups. They are then administered to a stratified, multistage probability sample. The students sampled are selected so that their assessment results may be generalized to the entire national population. Once the data have been collected, scored, and analyzed, NAEP publishes and disseminates the results. The objective is to provide information that will aid educators, legislators, and others to improve education in the United States. Questions used in the assessments are made available, with certain restrictions designed to protect their security, to states, localities, and researchers interested in using them.

To improve the usefulness of NAEP achievement results and provide the opportunity to examine policy issues, in recent assessments NAEP has asked numerous background questions. Students, teachers, and school officials answer a variety of questions about instruction, activities, experiences, curriculum, resources, attitudes, and demographics.

NAEP is supported by the Office for Educational Research and Improvement, Center for Statistics, in the U.S. Department of Education. In 1983, Educational Testing Service assumed responsibility for the administration of the project, which had previously been administered by the Education Commission of the States. NAEP is governed by an independent, legislatively defined board, the Assessment Policy Committee.

General Background About the 1983-84 NAEP Writing Assessment

There have been four national assessments of writing, the first in 1969-70 and subsequent ones in the 1973-74, 1978-79, and 1983-84 school years. Each has included an assessment of 9-, 13-, and 17-year-old students on a variety of open-ended writing tasks, with some of the tasks being readministered in successive assessments in order to gather some information about trends in writing performance over time.*

In 1983-84, NAEP began sampling students by grade as well as by age. The present report is based on the 1983-84 assessment of fourth, eighth, and eleventh graders attending public and private schools. Eighth graders were assessed in the fall (October-December), fourth graders in the winter (January-February), and eleventh graders in the spring (March-May).

The 1983-84 assessment included both reading and writing. Students at each grade level were administered from one to four out of a total of 15 writing tasks designed to measure performance on objectives developed by nationally representative panels of writing specialists, educators, and concerned citizens. The tasks were designed to include a range of reasons for writing, including informative, persuasive, and imaginative purposes. Although no individual student responded to all 15 tasks, each task was given to a national probability sample of approximately 2,000 students.

*See *Writing Trends Across the Decade, 1974-84*, National Assessment of Educational Progress, Educational Testing Service, 1986.

Students at each grade level also were asked numerous background questions about their writing practices and instruction, as well as their general background.

In order to describe the framework for the entire writing assessment, and therefore the context for reporting the results contained, the full text of one of the major objectives developed for the 1983-84 writing assessment, entitled "Students Use Writing to Accomplish a Variety of Purposes," is reproduced below.

Students Use Writing to Accomplish a Variety of Purposes*

Writing occurs regularly in people's personal and social lives as well as in school settings. People write to accomplish many different purposes, such as a letter to straighten out a billing error, a speech to explain a personal viewpoint on some issue, or a story for a school magazine. The ability to explain ideas to document events in writing can also help in a variety of job situations. Letters, reports, inventories, and a wide range of record keeping systems are integral to many businesses in today's "information society." Consequently, students need opportunities to develop a wide range of writing skills by writing for many purposes in varying contexts or situations.

In the sections that follow, three broadly inclusive purposes for writing are discussed: informative, persuasive, and literary. These purposes often blend into each other and vary in their mixtures according to the contexts for writing. For example, an autobiography might very well be considered literary, informative, and persuasive; a job application and resume may inform as well as persuade. Although these three purposes may frequently coexist in a piece of writing, one or another type may predominate. Writers' purposes are shaped by their initial perceptions of their topic, by the ways they consider their audience, by the social or instructional contexts in which they are writing, and by changes in focus that occur as their topic begins to develop a character of its own.

A. Informative Writing

Informative writing is used to share knowledge and convey messages, instructions, and ideas. Like all writing, informative writing is filtered through the writers' impressions, understandings, and feelings. Writing to inform others can involve reporting or retelling events or experiences that have happened. It can also involve analyzing or examining concepts and relationships or developing new hypotheses or generalizations from existing records, reports, and explanations. Depending on the demands of the task, the type of information and the context for writing, including the audience, writers may use one, several, or all of these skills.

*Writing Objectives, 1983-84 Assessment. National Assessment of Educational Progress, 1982.

90

B. Persuasive Writing

Persuasive writing attempts to bring about some action or change. Though it may begin in exploratory writing, and though it may contain great amounts of information—facts, details, examples, comparisons, statistics, or anecdotes—its aim is to influence others. Persuasive writing may entail responding to requests for advice by giving an opinion and supporting reasons. However, it usually involves initiating an attempt to convince readers by setting forth one's own point of view with evidence to back it up. Argument, with refutation, becomes part of persuasion when the writer knows there is opposition to what he or she is advocating. As such, persuasive writing must be concerned with the positions, beliefs, or attitudes of particular readers and with the possibility of winning their support or changing their beliefs or attitudes.

In all persuasive writing, writers must choose the stance they will take. They can, for instance, use emotional or logical appeals or an accommodating or demanding tone. Regardless of the situation or approach, writers must be concerned first with having an effect on readers, over and above merely adding to their knowledge of a particular topic.

C. Literary [Imaginative] Writing

Literary writing provides a special way of sharing our experiences and understanding the world. In this sense, literary writing shapes and expresses our thinking and feeling while contributing to our awareness of ourselves as makers, manipulators, and interpreters of reality. There is a wide variety of forms that literary writing can take, such as stories, poems, plays or song lyrics.

The term "literary" can also be used to define a motive or purpose for writing. The literary motive is evident whenever a writer's language breaks its conventional, "everyday" patterns in order to please or surprise, or when the language calls attention to itself and to the writer as a "shaper" or performer.

Literary language is difficult to catalog, but some conventional distinctions are illustrative: attention to rhythm and tone; the use of dialogue, story, and anecdote; the presence of metaphor, simile, and the less commonly labeled figures and tropes; the sense of play, pleasure, and surprise that is evident in a turn of phrase, a shift in plot, a line break, or an unexpected word or piece of punctuation. A persuasive statement, for example, can be convincing not only on the basis of its internal logic, but according to the strength of its illustrative material (its "stories"), its rhythm, the voice of its persona—all of those features that define the piece of writing as a performance on a page and not just a record of information.

The remaining NAEP 1983-84 writing assessment objectives discussed writing as a way of thinking and learning, managing the writing process, controlling language, and valuing writing.

Sampling

All NAEP assessments, including the 1983-84 reading and writing assessments, use a deeply stratified, multi-stage sampling design.* The first stage of sampling entails defining primary sampling units (PSUs)—typically counties, but sometimes aggregates of sparsely populated counties; classifying the PSUs into strata defined by region and community type; and randomly selecting PSUs. For each age/grade level, the second stage entails enumerating, stratifying, and randomly selecting schools, both public and private, within each PSU selected at the first stage. In 1983-84, 1,465 schools participated in the NAEP assessment—661 at grade 4, 478 at grade 8, and 326 at grade 11. The school cooperation rates were 88.6 percent at grade 4, 90.3 percent at grade 8, and 83.9 percent at grade 11.

The third stage of the sampling design involves randomly selecting students within a school for participation in NAEP. The 1983-84 assessment included 14,047 students at grade 4, 21,850 at grade 8, and 22,865 at grade 11. The student response rates were 91.3 percent, 87.3 percent and 82.8 percent at grades 4, 8, and 11, respectively. Some students sampled (less than 4 percent) were excluded because of limited English proficiency or a severe disability. In 1983-84, NAEP began collecting descriptive information about excluded students.

Balanced Incomplete Block (BIB) Spiralling

In the standard matrix sampling procedure formerly employed by NAEP, the total assessment battery, typically about six to seven hours of assessment material per subject, was divided into mutually exclusive booklets, each of which was allocated about 45 minutes of exercises. Since no student was administered more than one booklet, this simple matrix design allowed calculation of correlations and cross-tabulations among exercises within the same booklet but not among exercises in different booklets.

The new NAEP design instituted for the 1984 assessment remedies this deficiency by using a powerful variant of matrix sampling called BIB spiralling. With this procedure, the total assessment battery is divided into blocks of approximately 15 minutes each, and each student is administered a booklet containing three blocks as well as a six-minute block of background questions common to all students. Thus, the total assessment time for each student is still about the same.

The BIB (balanced incomplete block) part of the method assigns blocks of exercises to booklets in such a way that each block appears in the same number of booklets and each pair of blocks appears in at least one booklet. This generates a much larger number of different booklets. Fifty-seven different booklets for each grade level were required to administer the main part of the assessment in 1983-84. It should be noted that some writing tasks required a response time longer than the 15 minutes permitted in the BIB design. Thus, a portion of the 1983-84 writing assessment was administered in six additional booklets. These booklets allowed for the administration of "double blocks" of up to about 30 minutes of assessment time. These six booklets were spiralled along with the BIB booklets. The spiralling part of the method then cycles the booklets for administration so that typically no two students in any assessment session

*"Report on Sample Selection, Weighting and Variance Estimation, NAEP-Year 15," WESTAT, Inc., 1985.

in a school—and at most only a few students in schools with multiple sessions—receive the same booklet.

Using this procedure, each block of exercises was administered to approximately 2,000 students and each pair of blocks in the BIB portion of the assessment to about 200 students. Groups of about 12-25 students are assembled for assessment sessions, with each testing session lasting about one hour. This report is based on the 10,511 fourth graders, 11,492 eighth graders, and 12,028 eleventh graders who were administered writing tasks and background questions as part of the BIB assessment and the 6,476 fourth graders, 7,006 eighth graders, and 7,339 eleventh graders who wrote responses to tasks contained in the additional booklets.

Data Collection

NAEP assessments are always administered using a well-trained, professional data collection staff. WESTAT, Inc. was responsible for the 1983-84 assessment data collection. Quality control was provided through site visits by NAEP and WESTAT staff.

Primary Trait Scoring (Task Accomplishment)

The written responses discussed in this report were evaluated by trained readers using the primary trait scoring procedure.

The primary trait scoring guides were developed to focus raters' attention on how successfully each writing sample accomplished the rhetorical task specified by the writing prompt. This involved isolating particular features of the writing essential to accomplishing the task and developing criteria for various levels of performance based on those features. Papers were rated against these performance criteria, rather than in terms of relative quality within the population sampled. On a simple task, it is possible that all papers might be rated in the highest categories; on a difficult task, none might move out of the lowest categories.

In developing scoring guides, NAEP takes into account the constraints of the assessment situation. Samples of student performance represent their ability to produce first-draft writing on demand within a relatively short time under less than ideal conditions. The guidelines for evaluating task accomplishment reflect these limitations and do not require a finished performance.

For the exercises reported here, five levels of achievement were defined for each task: **not rated, unsatisfactory, minimal, adequate,** and **elaborated.** Responses **not rated** included those that were blank, off task, unreadable, or "I don't know." Across tasks, **unsatisfactory** responses were those that failed to reflect a basic understanding of the informative, persuasive, or imaginative purpose of the writing. **Minimal** responses recognized the elements needed to complete the task but were not managed well enough to insure the intended effect of the writing that resulted. **Adequate** responses included those features critical to accomplishing the underlying purpose; responses scored as **adequate** are likely to have the intended effect. **Elaborated** responses went beyond the merely **adequate,** reflecting a higher level of coherence and elaboration that is highly desirable, if not absolutely necessary.

A 20 percent random subsample of all the 1983-84 assessment responses was scored by a second rater to provide an estimate of interrater reliabilities for the primary

Percentages of Exact Score Point Agreemen
Primary Trait (Task Accomplishmen

Writing Tasks	GRADE 4	
	Percent Exact Agreement	Reliability Coefficient
Informative Writing		
Pets	92.3	.88
Job Application	—	—
Plants	92.1	.93
Appleby House	89.6	.92
XYZ Company	93.1	.92
Dali	90.9	.88
Favorite Music	93.4	.89
Food on the Frontier	92.5	.89
Persuasive Writing		
School Rule	91.6	.88
Dissecting Frogs	—	—
Swimming Pool	90.8	.89
Split Sessions	—	—
Spaceship	88.1	.90
Space Program	—	—
Recreation Opportunity	—	—
Radio Station	95.7	.97
Aunt May	91.6	.92
Uncle	—	—
Bike Lane	—	—
Imaginative Writing		
Hole in the Box	91.5	.89
Flashlight	92.9	.91
Ghost Story	93.3	.89

	GRADE 8		GRADE 11	
	Percent Exact Agreement	Reliability Coefficient	Percent Exact Agreement	Reliability Coefficient
	84.4	.78	—	—
	—	—	91.1	.92
	—	—	—	—
	79.0	.84	89.4	.92
	89.9	.86	—	—
	82.0	.81	91.3	.92
	84.4	.67	95.0	.90
	82.2	.76	92.6	.90
	81.4	.70	92.5	.91
	78.0	.71	—	—
	83.9	.82	90.9	.91
	84.4	.80	88.4	.88
	—	—	—	—
	—	—	90.2	.92
	86.4	.87	89.9	.92
	84.2	.88	—	—
	—	—	—	—
	—	—	89.3	.90
	—	—	88.5	.91
	82.6	.86	91.1	.92
	80.9	.79	92.3	.91
	83.1	.85	91.1	.93

trait scoring. **Table A.1** displays both the intraclass correlation and the percentage of exact score point ageement between first and second readers. The latter is displayed, since assessment results are presented by category or levels of achievement. By either measure, the rater reliabilities were very high. The somewhat lower reliabilities for eighth grade papers resulted because the administration in the fall preceded the assessment of the other grade levels and these responses were scored first. During the scoring of the eighth grade responses, NAEP instituted a computerized scorer reliability reporting system. This system provided data for each item and each reader on a weekly basis and, when it became fully operational, improved the reliability of the scoring. Thus, for grade 4 and 11 responses, most of the percentages of *exact* agreement are over 90 percent, and none are below 88 percent.

The Effect of Scoring Procedures on Comparisons Across Grade Levels

Since the responses to the 1983-84 writing assessment were evaluated as they were collected (age 13/grade 8 in the fall, age 9/grade 4 in the winter, and age 17/grade 11 in the spring), NAEP staff hypothesized that this procedure may have led to a "batch effect." That is, the age 9/grade 4 essays might have been evaluated too high, because after reading the essays written at age 13/grade 8, scorers may have found the grade 4 responses "pretty good" for fourth graders. Further, age 17/grade 11 responses may have been rated too low, because after the grade 4 responses, they may not have seemed "that good for an eleventh grader."

To determine the effect of scoring the papers in batches by age/grade levels, an experiment was performed in which NAEP written responses for all three grade levels were randomly ordered and then rescored. It was decided that if batch effects exceeding one-tenth of score point per item were found, *post hoc* adjustments of the writing scale values would be warranted.

The experiment was based on responses to three writing tasks that were administered to all three grade levels—School Rule, Food on the Frontier, and Swimming Pool. For each writing task at each age/grade level, a representative subsample of 156 to 174 papers was drawn. These numbers resulted in adequate statistical power without exceeding the resources available for rescoring the essays.

Because the booklets administered to each grade level were different colors, the responses were photocopied and then reordered using a randomly selected permutation of their sequence numbers. The responses were then scored by two experienced readers. The data were analyzed using repeated measures analysis of variance techniques. Estimates of the effects of batching ranged from .01 to .09. Since these effects were smaller than the *a priori* criterion value, NAEP concluded that it was not necessary to adjust writing scale values.

To improve the comparability of results obtained across grade levels, beginning with the 1986 assessment NAEP modified its design so that all three age/grade levels are assessed simultaneously in the spring. This also means that responses from the three age/grade levels of students now arrive back from the field together and are systematically intermingled before they are evaluated.

The Writing Scale: Average Response Method (ARM) Scaling

The IRT technology of NAEP's reading scale was not appropriate for the writing scale. For reading, there were a large number of exercises, of which 228 were used in the scale; and the individual exercises could be scored as right or wrong. For writing there were only 22 unique writing tasks across all three grade levels, of which only 10 were useful for the writing scale; and the individual exercises were evaluated on a 0-4 scale. Several attempts were made to adopt IRT technology to these non-binary writing exercise responses, but these efforts have not yet proved fruitful.

Writing Tasks Included in the 1984 NAEP Writing Assessment

Writing Tasks	GRADE 4	GRADE 8	GRADE 11
Informative Writing			
Pets*	X	X	
Job Application			X
Plants	X		
Appleby House*	X	X	X
XYZ Company*	X	X	
Dali*	X	X	X
Favorite Music	X	X	X
Food on the Frontier*	X	X	X
Persuasive Writing			
School Rule*	X	X	X
Dissecting Frogs*		X	
Swimming Pool*	X	X	X
Split Sessions		X	X
Spaceship	X		
Space Program			X
Recreation Opportunity*		X	X
Radio Station*	X	X	
Aunt May	X		
Uncle			X
Bike Lane			X
Imaginative Writing			
Hole in the Box	X	X	X
Flashlight	X	X	X
Ghost Story	X	X	X

*Included in the writing scale.

NAEP's writing scale ranges from 0 to 400 and is defined as the average of a respondent's scores on 10 specific tasks.* These 10 were selected because they were included in the BIB-spiralled portion of the assessment and tended to be given at more than one grade level. BIB spiralling has the property of assuring that each pair of exercises is administered to a randomly equivalent subsample of students. Thus, all the intercorrelations among these essays were able to be estimated. Since the remaining writing tasks were in the six additional non-BIB booklets and only linked to the BIB portion of the assessment through reading blocks, it was not possible at this time to develop the technology necessary to extend the scale to include all 22 writing tasks.

All the exercises included in the 1983-84 writing assessment are shown in **Table A.2.** Those included in the scale are marked with an asterisk(*). Nine of the 10 asterisked tasks were administered at more than one grade level. The entire set of 10 tasks was assessed in the eighth grade, while eight of the tasks were administered to students in the fourth grade and six to students in the eleventh grade. Nine of the tasks were given to at least two grades, with information on five of the tasks obtained from all three grades. (Although Dissecting Frogs was only given at eighth grade, it was included in the scale because it was in the same block as XYZ Company, which was also given at fourth grade.)

As indicated previously, not every student responded to every writing task. Of the approximately 10,000 students in each grade level who participated in the BIB portion of the 1983-84 assessment and were given at least one writing task, the majority were given only one or two, and none were given more than four. Thus, the writing scale score is a latent variable, and the average over all 10 writing tasks had to be estimated.

Using the ARM scaling method, NAEP computed values for each of the 8,807 fourth graders, 11,092 eighth graders, and 12,028 eleventh graders who had responded to at least one of the 10 writing tasks. (Of these students, about 2,000 at a given grade responded to a particular item, and about 200 responded to a given pair of tasks.)

The basis for estimation of a predicted value for any given student is the full cross-products matrix

$$
C = \begin{vmatrix} X'X & X'Z \\ Z'X & Z'Z \end{vmatrix}
$$

from which all other necessary matrices and estimates are derived. For the construction of the NAEP writing scale, this Matrix C was formed by creating an analogous matrix for each grade and then pooling by adding the resulting matrices together.

*Technical Report of NAEP's 1983-84 Assessment, National Assessment of Educational Progress, Educational Testing Service.

Z is a matrix for the writing scores of the subjects on the writing essays. X is a matrix containing the values of the conditioning variables for the students. To improve the estimates of achievement, the NAEP scaling procedure uses other available information in the estimation process. In the matrix C, and in the grade analogues C4, C8, and C11, the conditioning matrix X specifically controls for the main effects of the following conditioning variables:

Grade: grade 4, grade 8, grade 11
Sex: male, female
Race/Ethnicity: White, Black, Hispanic, Other
Size/Type of Community: urban-disadvantaged, urban-advantaged, other
Region: Northeast, Southeast, Central, West
Parental Education: less than high school, graduated high school, post-high-school, unknown

The values of the conditioning variables are known for all students; and X′X in each of the cross-products matrices is directly obtained by taking the sum of squares and cross-products of the conditioning variables for each student, weighting these by the student's sampling weight, and then summing across all students of the given grade.

Because no student took all of the writing tasks, the matrix Z′Z could not be directly obtained. However, the BIB spiralling procedure produces sufficient information to estimate the mean and standard deviation of each writing score and also the correlation between each pair of scores. Furthermore, because the BIB spiralling procedure presents items and pairs of items to randomly equivalent (i.e., representative) subsamples, estimates of means, variances, and covariances, based on the total set of available responses, are unbiased for the population values. These means, variances, and correlations are used to build up consistent estimators of the cross-product matrices Z′Z and X′Z for all items assigned within a grade. Since all items were presented in the eighth grade, this resulted in a consistent estimate of the complete cross-product matrix C8.

Because not all writing tasks were given at grades 4 and 11, the cross-product matrices, C4 and C11, had missing cells. Grade 4 had two missing items and grade 11 had four missing items. The cells of these matrices (which included all sums of cross-products involving missing items) were filled in by: 1) assuming that, for the population of fourth- or eleventh-grade students respectively, the conditional distribution of the missing items given the background characteristics and responses to the items actually assigned is the same as the equivalent conditional distribution for the population of eighth grade students, and is multivariate normal, 2) estimating the conditional distribution for the eighth grade sample, and then 3) combining the estimate with the marginal distribution obtained from the fourth or eleventh grade normal equations to obtain an estimate of the joint distributions of all items for each population of students (fourth and eleventh graders).

In summary, the ARM procedure for estimating average writing achievement provides an estimate of average achievement for each respondent as if each had taken all ten writing tasks and NAEP had computed average achievement across those ten tasks. More specifically, the ARM scale gives an estimate of average achievement for performance on the ten tasks which were actually administered to eighth graders as part of the fully BIBed part of the 1983-84 assessment. This predicted mean score on the ten items was derived based on each individual's item responses and on selected demographic characteristics. The student responses to the writing tasks were coded: 0 = Not Rated, 1 = Unsatisfactory, 2 = Minimal, 3 = Adequate, and 4 = Elaborated. The averages have been multiplied by 100 for ease of reporting.

The ARM estimates of average writing achievement have the very advantageous

Average Writing Achievement for NAEP Subgroups

	GRADES					
	4		**8**		**11**	
	ARM	Mean 15 Tasks	ARM	Mean 15 Tasks	ARM	Mean 15 Tasks
Nation	158 (1)	167 (1)	205 (1)	200 (1)	219 (1)	208 (1)
Race/Ethnicity						
Black	138 (2)	143 (2)	186 (1)	180 (2)	200 (2)	189 (2)
Hispanic	146 (2)	157 (2)	187 (2)	182 (2)	200 (2)	189 (2)
Asian-American	163 (4)	177 (4)	211 (4)	214 (2)	219 (4)	206 (3)
White	163 (1)	173 (1)	211 (1)	206 (1)	224 (1)	214 (1)
Sex						
Male	150 (1)	160 (1)	196 (1)	190 (1)	209 (1)	197 (1)
Female	166 (1)	174 (1)	214 (1)	210 (1)	229 (1)	219 (1)
Region						
Northeast	161 (2)	172 (2)	209 (1)	205 (2)	222 (3)	211 (3)
Southeast	154 (2)	161 (3)	203 (2)	198 (3)	216 (2)	206 (2)
Central	160 (2)	168 (2)	206 (1)	199 (2)	220 (2)	210 (3)
West	157 (1)	167 (2)	203 (2)	199 (2)	217 (1)	206 (1)
Size/Type Community						
Rural	153 (2)	153 (4)	203 (3)	194 (4)	213 (3)	202 (5)
Disadvan.-Urban	142 (2)	149 (2)	188 (2)	185 (2)	201 (2)	189 (4)
Advan.-Urban	170 (2)	182 (3)	221 (2)	221 (2)	228 (2)	214 (4)
Parents Level of Ed.						
No H. S. diploma	143 (3)	152 (3)	189 (2)	284 (2)	199 (2)	192 (2)
Grad. high school	154 (1)	164 (2)	202 (1)	198 (1)	215 (1)	204 (1)
Post-high-school	166 (1)	176 (1)	213 (1)	209 (2)	227 (1)	216 (1)
Reading Materials in the Home						
0-2	147 (1)	146 (2)	186 (2)	173 (2)	197 (3)	176 (3)
3	154 (2)	161 (1)	198 (1)	189 (2)	205 (2)	189 (2)
4	159 (2)	170 (2)	203 (1)	197 (1)	216 (1)	204 (1)
5	164 (1)	179 (1)	210 (1)	208 (1)	223 (1)	214 (1)

property of being comparable across grade levels and, therefore, providing information about growth across years of schooling. The disadvantage of this procedure is that, like all multiple regression techniques, ARM scaling can yield attenuated results. Therefore, NAEP became concerned about the magnitude of regression toward the national means in the computation of the means for the various subpopulations of students, specifically for subgroups not included in the conditioning matrix. In addition, in using the ARM scaling methodology to estimate average writing performance, NAEP estimated an achievement distribution for each individual and then selected five random values from that distribution, each of which can be used as an estimate of that student's

| | GRADES | | | | | |
| | 4 | | 8 | | 11 | |
	ARM	Mean 15 Tasks	ARM	Mean 15 Tasks	ARM	Mean 15 Tasks
Mothers Working Outside Home						
Yes	160 (1)	170 (1)	206 (1)	201 (1)	220 (1)	209 (2)
No	156 (1)	164 (1)	205 (1)	199 (1)	217 (1)	206 (1)
Do you have a computer in your home?						
Yes	160 (1)	170 (1)	207 (1)	203 (2)	221 (1)	211 (2)
No	158 (1)	167 (1)	205 (1)	200 (1)	218 (1)	207 (1)
Do you ever use a computer to write stories, papers, or letters*						
Yes	151 (5)	163 (7)	204 (4)	197 (5)	223 (4)	220 (3)
No	161 (3)	172 (2)	206 (2)	204 (2)	218 (2)	213 (2)
Hours of TV Viewing						
0-2 Hours	164 (1)	176 (2)	211 (1)	209 (1)	222 (1)	213 (1)
3-5 Hours	160 (1)	172 (2)	207 (1)	204 (1)	216 (1)	207 (1)
6 Hours or More	150 (2)	154 (1)	196 (2)	185 (1)	207 (2)	187 (2)
Homework						
None assigned	158 (1)	169 (2)	203 (1)	198 (2)	213 (1)	196 (1)
Did not do it	150 (2)	146 (3)	196 (3)	182 (3)	214 (2)	195 (2)
Less than 1 Hour	159 (1)	170 (1)	207 (1)	203 (1)	218 (1)	210 (1)
1-2 Hours	162 (1)	173 (2)	210 (1)	207 (1)	222 (1)	216 (1)
More than 2 Hours	153 (3)	157 (3)	207 (2)	204 (2)	227 (2)	221 (2)
Pages read for school or homework						
5	155 (1)	161 (2)	201 (2)	193 (1)	213 (2)	193 (2)
6-10	160 (2)	170 (2)	207 (1)	202 (1)	217 (1)	207 (1)
11-15	161 (1)	175 (2)	210 (1)	208 (1)	220 (2)	213 (2)
16-20	160 (2)	172 (2)	209 (2)	207 (2)	221 (2)	213 (2)
More than 20	158 (2)	169 (1)	205 (2)	201 (2)	223 (2)	215 (2)

*Means based on 11 rather than 15 tasks, since this question was not paired with all writing tasks.

average writing achievement. Using these values provides more appropriate estimates of group means and their variability, but they are not optimal estimates of individual achievement for relational analyses. Since NAEP used these values as the measure of student achievement in the relational analyses, there was further concern that the results might be further attenuated and relationships might be seriously understated.

In order to judge the extent of the attenuation in subgroup differences, NAEP also estimated average writing achievement based on the observed sample means of each

Average Writing Achievement

| | GRADES | | | | | |
| | 4 | | 8 | | 11 | |
	ARM	Mean 10 Tasks	ARM	Mean 10 Tasks	ARM	Mean 10 Tasks
Values Writing						
Low	159 (2)	169 (2)	202 (1)	200 (2)	214 (1)	204 (2)
Medium	157 (1)	169 (2)	207 (2)	209 (2)	219 (1)	215 (2)
High	157 (1)	171 (2)	206 (1)	207 (2)	223 (2)	221 (2)
Attitude Toward Writing						
Low	156 (2)	167 (3)	202 (1)	200 (2)	216 (2)	203 (2)
Medium	159 (2)	172 (2)	208 (1)	210 (1)	220 (1)	216 (2)
High	155 (3)	161 (3)	205 (2)	210 (4)	222 (4)	218 (4)
Writing for Personal Purposes						
Low	156 (2)	168 (2)	197 (1)	195 (2)	212 (2)	202 (3)
Medium	158 (1)	171 (1)	206 (1)	206 (1)	218 (1)	214 (1)
High	159 (1)	166 (2)	210 (1)	209 (2)	226 (1)	220 (2)
Writing for Functional Purposes						
Low	161 (3)	178 (3)	204 (1)	203 (2)	217 (1)	210 (2)
Medium	161 (1)	174 (1)	208 (1)	209 (1)	220 (1)	217 (1)
High	151 (2)	157 (2)	203 (2)	202 (2)	220 (2)	213 (3)
Sharing Work with Others						
Low	158 (3)	168 (3)	200 (2)	198 (3)	217 (2)	206 (3)
Medium	160 (1)	178 (2)	206 (2)	205 (3)	218 (2)	210 (5)
High	156 (2)	163 (3)	208 (2)	212 (4)	222 (3)	214 (5)
Use of Planning Strategies						
Low	157 (2)	168 (5)	203 (2)	200 (4)	211 (2)	196 (4)
Medium	158 (3)	174 (4)	205 (2)	204 (3)	218 (2)	209 (4)
High	158 (2)	171 (4)	206 (1)	208 (3)	221 (2)	214 (4)
Use of Revising and Editing Strategies						
Low	156 (1)	168 (2)	199 (2)	193 (2)	209 (2)	188 (3)
Medium	157 (1)	168 (2)	203 (1)	202 (2)	215 (1)	206 (2)
High	163 (2)	174 (3)	212 (1)	214 (2)	224 (1)	220 (2)

grade level across each of the 15 separate writing tasks administered to that grade level. Since a nationally representative sample of 2,000 students at any given grade level responded to each of the 15 writing tasks administered to that grade level, the mean performance level was first obtained for each task administered to that grade level. The average of the observed sample means for each of the tasks is then an unbiased estimate of average student performance at the grade level on those 15 writing tasks. The same procedure also was used to compute average writing achievement across

For Writing Background Factors

TABLE A.4

	GRADES					
	4		**8**		**11**	
	ARM	Mean 10 Tasks	ARM	Mean 10 Tasks	ARM	Mean 10 Tasks
Number of Reports and Essays						
0	156 (3)	166 (5)	193 (3)	191 (3)	208 (4)	211 (5)
1-2	160 (3)	179 (3)	203 (2)	202 (3)	219 (2)	216 (3)
3-4	163 (4)	180 (5)	210 (2)	210 (4)	222 (2)	223 (4)
5-10	161 (3)	184 (5)	209 (2)	212 (5)	223 (2)	220 (3)
11 or more	160 (4)	177 (4)	209 (3)	210 (4)	218 (5)	220 (6)
Writing in English Class						
Low	161 (1)	175 (1)	208 (1)	209 (1)	221 (1)	217 (2)
Medium	159 (1)	171 (2)	207 (1)	207 (2)	220 (1)	214 (1)
High	153 (2)	159 (2)	202 (1)	200 (2)	213 (2)	203 (2)
Process-Oriented Teaching Activities						
Low	160 (2)	177 (2)	204 (1)	200 (2)	216 (2)	210 (4)
Medium	158 (2)	170 (3)	207 (1)	208 (2)	220 (1)	215 (1)
High	152 (3)	158 (4)	203 (2)	202 (3)	220 (2)	216 (2)
Teacher Comments on Final Paper						
Low	163 (4)	185 (4)	209 (2)	210 (3)	220 (2)	217 (4)
Medium	157 (2)	170 (4)	203 (2)	200 (3)	220 (2)	217 (3)
High	155 (2)	166 (2)	203 (2)	205 (2)	216 (2)	211 (3)
Teacher Feedback						
Low	158 (1)	170 (4)	202 (1)	197 (2)	217 (2)	195 (3)
Medium	157 (2)	167 (3)	206 (1)	208 (3)	218 (2)	208 (2)
High	158 (3)	168 (5)	205 (2)	203 (3)	219 (2)	218 (3)
Reading Proficiency*						
Rudimentary	133 (4)	115 (6)	—	—	—	—
Basic	145 (1)	142 (2)	177 (3)	157 (4)	183 (5)	147 (1)
Intermediate	160 (1)	174 (1)	195 (1)	188 (1)	202 (2)	177 (2)
Adept	171 (2)	197 (2)	210 (1)	212 (1)	216 (1)	209 (1)
Advanced	180 (6)	208 (7)	222 (2)	231 (2)	227 (1)	229 (2)

*Results are not presented for the rudimentary reading proficiency level at grades 8 and 11, because all but a few (0.2 percent) eighth graders and all eleventh graders attained at least the basic level of reading proficiency.

the 15 tasks for each of NAEP's subpopulations. Finally, the same procedure was used to obtain observed sample means for the low, medium, and high groupings on each of the writing background factors across the 10 writing tasks administered to each of the grade levels as part of the fully BIBed portion of the 1983-84 writing assessment. These results are based on the 10 tasks given to each grade level as part of the BIB portion of the assessment, because only questions in that portion of the assessment could be used to assign factor scores (see the section on Background Factors found later in this Procedural Appendix).

The difficulty with the estimates based on the observed sample means is grounded in the fact that each grade level was given a partially overlapping but different set of writing tasks. This enabled NAEP to administer some writing tasks that seemed more appropriate for students in upper or lower grades. Thus, some easier writing tasks were given to the fourth grade students and some more difficult tasks to the eleventh grade students. As a consequence of the different difficulty levels of the different sets of tasks given to each grade level, interpretations of grade level differences in performance are confounded.

The results for average writing achievement as computed by both methods and their standard errors are presented in **Tables A.3** and **A.4.** Table A.3 displays the results for subgroups that could be defined for the entire NAEP sample, those based on questions included in each booklet. Table A.4 displays the results for subgroups that were defined based on questions in the BIB portion of the assessment. The results from the two different computations are quite consistent. While there is some attenuation in the ARM estimates, it is generally slight. However, on occasion these slight variations in result also suggest different directions for relationships. Given that the ARM estimates enable comparisons across grade levels and the means of observed performance do not, NAEP elected to base this report on the ARM results, but to note discrepancies in the results obtained from the two methods.

NAEP Reporting Groups

NAEP does not report results for individual students. It only reports performance for groups of students. Information about region and size/type of community was obtained from the sampling frame, sex of the students from school records, and reading proficiency levels from the reading assessment. Other group results are based on student answers to the common core of questions administered to all students. In addition to national results, this report contains information about subgroups defined by race/ethnicity, sex, region of the country, size/type of community, level of reading proficiency, level of parents' education, reading materials in the home, mothers working outside the home, computer in the home, use of a computer to write, television viewing, homework, and pages read for homework. Definitions of these groups follow.

Race/Ethnicity

Results are presented for Black, White, Hispanic, and Asian-American students. Results for other racial/ethnic groups are not reported because the sample sizes are not large enough to provide reliable results. Results are based on student reports to the two following questions:

1. Are you

    A. American Indian or Alaskan Native
    B. Asian or Pacific Islander
    C. Black
    D. White
    E. Other (What?) _____

2. Are you Hispanic?

    A. No
    B. Yes, Mexican, Mexican American, or Chicano
    C. Yes, Puerto Rican
    D. Yes, Cuban
    E. Yes, other Spanish/Hispanic (What?) _____

Students responding "yes" were classified as Hispanic.

Sex

Results are reported for males and females.

Region

The country has been divided into four regions: Northeast, Southeast, Central, and West. States included in each region are shown on the map below.

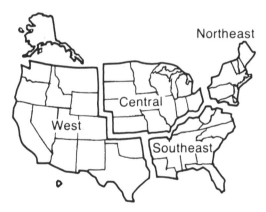

Size/Type of Community

Three extreme community types of special interest are defined by an occupational profile of the area served by a school as well as by the size of the community in which the school is located. This is the only reporting category that excludes a large number of respondents. About two-thirds do not fall into the classifications listed below. Results for the remaining two-thirds are not reported in this breakdown, since their performance was similar to that of the nation.

Advantaged-urban (high-metro) communities. Students in this group attend schools in or around cities having a population greater than 200,000 where a high proportion of the residents are in professional or managerial positions.

Disadvantaged-urban (low-metro) communities. Students in this group attend schools in or around cities having a population greater than 200,000 where a high proportion of the residents are receiving government assistance or are not regularly employed.

Rural communities. Students in this group attend schools in areas with a population under 10,000, where many of the residents are farmers or farm workers.

Levels of Reading Proficiency

NAEP reported the results of the 1983-84 reading assessment on an IRT scale ranging from 0 to 500. To aid in interpreting the results, NAEP also described what readers at different proficiency levels were able to do. The description of each level was based on the assessment results and reflects the interaction of the varieties of types of knowledge, skills, and strategies that together comprise successful reading at each level. Five levels of reading proficiency were identified: rudimentary (150), basic (200), intermediate (250), adept (300), and advanced (350). Writing achievement results are presented for students attaining each level of reading proficiency, but not the next highest level. The one exception was that the few fourth graders who did not attain the rudimentary level were included with those who did. Therefore, this category (which only occurs at fourth grade) includes the few students (about 3 percent) with reading proficiency levels from 0 to 199. The basic level includes those students from 200 to 249, intermediate from 250 to 299, adept from 300 to 349, and advanced 350 and above.

Level of Parental Education

National Assessment defines three categories of parental education levels, based on students' reports. These categories are: (1) those whose parents did not graduate from high school, (2) those who have at least one parent who graduated from high school, and (3) those who have at least one parent who has had some post-high school education.

Reading Materials in the Home

Students at all three ages were asked: (1) Does your family get a newspaper regularly? (2) Is there an encyclopedia in your home? (3) Are there more than 25 books in your home? (4) Does your family get any magazines regularly? (5) Is there a dictionary in your home? Results are provided for 0-2 "yes" responses, as well as for three, four, and five "yes" responses.

Mothers Working Outside the Home

NAEP asked students: Does your mother work outside your home? Results are presented for students who answered "yes" and for those who answered "no."

Computer in the Home

NAEP asked students: Is there a computer in your home? Results are presented for students who answered "yes" and for those who answered "no."

Use of Computer to Write

NAEP asked a subsample of the respondents: Do you ever use a computer to write stories, papers, or letters? Results are presented for students who answered "yes" and for those who answered "no."

Television Viewing

Students were asked: How much television do you usually watch each day? Results are reported for those responding two hours or less, three to five hours, and six hours or more.

Homework

Students were asked: How much time did you spend on homework yesterday?
A. No homework was assigned.
B. I had homework but didn't do it.
C. Less than 1 hour
D. 1-2 hours
E. More than 2 hours
Results are reported for each response.

Pages Read for Homework

NAEP asked students: About how many pages a day do you have to read in school and for homework? The response options included: More than 20, 16-20, 11-15, 6-10, and 5 or fewer. Results are reported for each response.

The Writing Background Factors

In addition to those background questions in the common core administered to all the students in the sample, NAEP also asked 109 questions specific to writing practice and instruction. These questions were included in the writing blocks in the BIB portion of the assessment. Thus, like the writing tasks included in that portion of the assessment, each question was given to 2,000 students and each pair of questions was given to a randomly equivalent subsample of students. As with the writing tasks in the BIB portion of the assessment, it was possible to use the ARM procedure to estimate responses. Here, all questions were given to students at all three grade levels.

NAEP initiated the process of developing composite variables for the background factors related to writing achievement by conducting a factor analysis of the results to the 109 questions for each of the three grade levels separately. Although a few differences occurred, the majority of the factors were very similar across the three grades. For ease of reporting and interpretation, NAEP reran the factor analysis for all three grade levels combined.

The missing data covariance matrices for each grade were pooled and then a correlation matrix of 109 questions was computed. This matrix was factored using principal components with unities in the diagonal. The latent roots were examined and it was decided to rotate 10 factors. The 10 factors were rotated orthogonally to a varimax solution. These results were examined and in the process of assigning questions to unique factors, two new factors were created and one was deleted.

This process eventually resulted in the 11 factor scales reported in Part II of this report. These factors are based on 98 background questions. The factors were standardized on a 5-point scale by truncating each score back to the preceding whole number (0-.99 = 0, 1.00-1.99 = 1, 2.00-2.99 = 2, 3.00-3.99 = 3, and 4.00 and above = 4) and then adding 1 to each value. Since very few students fell at the extremes of the distributions for each of the factors, the results were collapsed as follows: Low as 1 and 2, Moderate as 3, and High as 4 and 5.

The factors and the questions that comprise them are listed below:

Factor 1. Value Placed on Writing

How often is each of the following true?

1. Writing is important.
2. Writing helps me learn about myself.
3. Writing helps me remind myself and others about things.
4. Writing helps me study.
5. Writing helps me come up with new ideas.
6. People who write well have a better chance of getting good jobs than people who don't write well.
7. People who write well are more influential than people who don't write well.
8. Writing helps me to think more clearly.
9. Writing helps me tell others what I think.
10. Writing helps me tell others how I feel about things.
11. Writing helps me to understand my own feelings about things.
12. Writing can help me get a good job.
13. Writing helps me share my ideas.
14. Writing helps me show people that I know something.

Factor 2. Extent of Teacher Focus on Final Product

After you have written papers, how often does the teacher talk or write to you about each of the following things?

1. How you followed directions
2. Whether you wrote enough in your paper
3. The ideas in your paper
4. The way you explained your ideas
5. The way you expressed your feelings
6. The way you organized your paper
7. The words that you used
8. Your spelling, punctuation, and grammar
9. Your neatness and handwriting

Factor 3. Use of Revising and Editing Strategies

How often do you do each of the following to make your papers better?

1. Move some sentences or paragraphs to different parts of the paper
2. Add new ideas or information
3. Take out parts of the paper that you don't like
4. Change some words for other words that you like better
5. Correct mistakes in spelling
6. Correct mistakes in grammar
7. Correct mistakes in punctuation
8. Rewrite almost all of the paper
9. Throw out the first paper and start again

How often when you write papers do you do each of the following?

10. Think about where different facts or ideas should go in the paper
11. Make changes as you write
12. Make changes after you have written the paper once

The following questions ask about the last thing that you wrote in school.

13. Did you copy over what you wrote before handing it in?
14. Did you make changes in what you wrote?

Factor 4. Student and People Student Lives with Use Writing for Functional Purposes

How often do the people you live with do each of the following?

1. Make lists of things to buy or do
2. Copy recipes or directions for making things
3. Fill out order blanks to buy things
4. Work crossword puzzles or play word games
5. Write stories or poems

How often do you do each of the following?

6. Make lists of things to buy or do
7. Copy recipes or directions for making things
8. Fill out order blanks to buy things
9. Help other students with their writing
10. Write about something you have read
11. Write papers that you think are good but are too personal to show to anyone
12. Write for the school newspaper, magazine, or yearbook

Do you ever use a computer to do the following?

13. Write stories, papers, or letters

Factor 5. Extent of Process-Oriented Teaching Activities

How often when you are writing papers does your teacher ask you to do each of the following?

1. Make notes before you write
2. Make an outline for the paper
3. Make notes for yourself about changes in the paper
4. Talk with the teacher about the paper while you are working on it
5. Talk with some classmates about the paper while you are working on it
6. Write the paper more than once before it is graded
7. Work on the paper again after it has been graded

How often do you do each of the following things when you study for a test?

8. Take notes on what you read
9. Make outlines of what you read

Factor 6. Student and People Student Lives with Use Writing for Personal/Social Purposes

1. How many times during last week did you write something that was NOT a school assignment?

How often do the people you live with do the following?

2. Keep diaries or journals
3. Write letters to friends or relatives
4. Write notes and messages

How often do you do each of the following?

    5. Keep a diary or journal
    6. Write letters to friends or relatives
    7. Write notes and messages
    8. Write stories or poems that are not schoolwork

How often is the following true for you?

    9. Writing helps me keep in touch with friends

When you have free time, how often do you do each of the following?

    10. Write in a diary or journal
    11. Write a letter

Factor 7. Attitude Toward Writing

How often is each of the following true?

    1. I like to write.
    2. I am a good writer
    3. I think writing is a waste of time.
    4. People like what I write.
    5. I write on my own outside the school.
    6. I don't like to write things that will be graded.
    7. If I didn't have to write for school, I wouldn't write anything.

The following question asks about the last thing that you wrote in school.

    8. Did you like doing the writing?

Factor 8. Teacher Feedback

How often does the teacher do each of the following things with your writing?

    1. Mark the mistakes in your paper
    2. Write notes on your paper
    3. Point out what you did well
    4. Point out what you did not do well
    5. Make suggestions about what you should do the next time you write
    6. Show an interest in what you write

Factor 9. Number of Pieces of Writing in English Class

About how many of each of the following kinds of writing did you do for your English class last week?

    1. A story
    2. An essay, composition, or theme
    3. A poem
    4. A play
    5. A letter
    6. A book report
    7. Another kind of report

Factor 10. Use of Planning Strategies

How often when you write papers do you do each of the following?

    1. Think about what you want to say before you start writing.
    2. Ask yourself what kinds of things people would like to know about the subject of the paper.
    3. Look up facts in books, magazines, or newspapers.
    4. Write in different ways for different people.